EVERYBODY WINS

EVERY BODY WINS

The Story Behind the Ungame®

Rhea Zakich

Tyndale House
Publishers, Inc.
Wheaton, Illinois

Library of Congress
Catalog Card Number
79-65028

ISBN 0-8423-0788-5,
cloth

First printing,
September 1979.

Printed in the United
States of America.

PART ONE
The Inner City

CHAPTER 1

By the time I was thirty I had fulfilled all the dreams I had had as a young girl. In my teen-age years I thought that the ultimate was to be married to a nice handsome man who made good money. I would have two healthy children, live in an attractive house in a desirable neighborhood, and have lots of friends. Owning two cars was almost unheard of in those days, so I thought that my dream was really far out: to have two cars.

On the night of my thirtieth birthday, I became aware that my dream was real. I had attained every goal I had set for myself. But was that all there was? I sensed no excitement at having "arrived."

Up to this time in my life I had prided myself on being a fantastic mother. I kept the house neat and clean, and things ran smoothly. My two sons, Darin and Dean, were preschoolers and I spent my days with them, meeting their needs. I thought the best mother in the world was one who took her children to the doctor for their checkups, gave them vitamins, read them bedtime stories, pulled them in the wagon, put color-coordinated clothes on them, and sang to them. I was able even to anticipate things before they happened and take proper action. That's what I thought every mother was to strive for. On the eve of my birthday it dawned on me that my life was monotonous.

Everything was predictable. There were no highs or lows, and such a state was boring.

Of course I couldn't tell anyone I felt bored because I was always doing something. I was active in my church: choir, Sunday school, committees, women's group. I had been in a prayer group which seemed to meet my needs, at least until now. I drove my boys to nursery school every day (one went on Monday, Wednesday, Friday; the other on Tuesday, Thursday). So how could I be bored?

I lay there in bed and thought, "If I only live to age sixty; my life is half over." What had I done? What difference did it make to anyone that I had lived? Oh, I'd given birth to two babies, but who couldn't do that? I felt insignificant, as if I was missing something. Do other women feel this way? I wondered.

Eventually I fell asleep, not realizing that my questions had opened the door to my answers. My life was beginning to change, though I didn't know it. Tomorrow would be a new beginning.

The next day I went to my prayer group at the United Methodist Church, as I had every Monday morning for nearly two years. I enjoyed discussing God, the Scriptures, Jesus, prayer, and books on those subjects. I'd been content to exchange opinions, recipes, the latest gossip.

Why did today seem different? Why was it irritating me to hear the same topics being hashed over again? What was this hollow feeling in me that seemed to be a hunger for something more? What was this itch that made me want to get up and *do* something instead of just sit there and talk about it? I couldn't understand what was wrong (right?) with me.

As the women compared theologies on a certain chapter of the Bible, I felt as if I wanted to scream. "Hey, we've been talking about that for months! Why don't we do something?" We'd read about the miracles Jesus performed: walking on the water, raising Lazarus from the dead, healing sick people, calming the wind. We'd read that we could do those things—and even *greater things*. And then everybody turns the page and says "Let's go on to the next chapter."

Why can't I say something? Why am I just sitting here? I imagined myself shouting, "Stop! Why don't we put down our books for a minute and figure out how *we* can do these things? If we can *do* them, what are we doing just reading books about them?" I opened my mouth and all that came out was "Don't you think it would be fun to try some of these things?" How dumb. Why didn't I say what I was feeling? A little later I tried again. I suggested that perhaps we could get a prayer project. Everyone looked at me as if I was disrupting the class.

So I returned to my Southern California tract home with its neatly manicured lawn in a walled-in neighborhood in upper-middle-class white suburbia and worked on a bazaar project and hoped that the feelings would go away. I felt guilty that I didn't feel more appreciative of all the advantages in my life. I had done nothing to earn where I was. I just woke up and found myself here. I supposed that millions of people would gladly take my place. Why wasn't I happy about where I was?

I had come from an average family made up of both parents, three brothers, and a kid sister. Being born near the end of the Depression years, I recall my dad having to work long hours to make ends meet. When I think of how hard my mother, too, seemed to work raising us five kids, I know she probably dreamed of this place where I now found myself. It would have seemed like heaven to her. I don't remember needing things that I didn't eventually get (wanting them, yes, but not needing them).

My family stayed to themselves, never asking for assistance or help, maybe in a way proud of managing and coping. I always felt safe and secure, even in those frightening thunderstorms and tornados that occasionally sweep through Ohio. I could see how my childhood and upbringing had influenced my life now. My husband Dan and I had built the same kind of safe haven for our children and had done so independent of any help. Ah! I'm beginning to sense why it seems so different for us than it probably did for my parents. They probably had great feelings of accomplishment and satisfaction to have been able to hold their head high during that time when survival was not easy. They probably had worthy goals, like getting through

the week. Each year saw them closer to the end of the
rough times, when they might be able to save enough
money for a vacation. Putting five kids through school was
something to be proud of, I suppose. Yes, it would have
been different for them.

I began to see why there was no great exhilaration
about where Dan and I were. First of all, we never had to
struggle. Dan had had a good job ever since we got married and we had money in the bank. He has a good
education so the fear of being out of work was not a part
of our life. (Little did we know that in a few years we, too,
were to experience some of the "joys" of unemployment
and struggling.)

We had never even talked about goals. Oh, we might
have decided that next year we would get new carpeting
or trade in a car, but we had no high hopes or aspirations.
"Maintain" was our middle name.

At this same time in our life, but seemingly far removed
from us, a town was on fire. The Watts riots broke out one
week after my birthday in 1965. I remember the special
news bulletins on TV saying that another fire had erupted.
There were scenes of people running and firemen rushing
to spray a little stream of water on a collapsing building.
All of that had nothing to do with us, or at least I didn't
think it did. I'd never heard of Watts, even though I found
out later that it's only about thirty-five miles from our
home. I couldn't imagine why people would behave like
that and I certainly didn't know what could be done about
it.

I became bored with the TV coverage and usually used
the time during news bulletins to go to the refrigerator for
a snack. I had no idea that the rioting would affect me in
any way.

After a few days the television stations began to show
live coverage all day. My two daytime serials were pre-
empted. How dare they do such a thing! I'd been watching
"Young Doctor Malone" and "As the World Turns" for
years. The mood of my whole day was determined by
those programs. What right did they have to hog up all the

stations for something that didn't have anything to do with "Us"! If those people want to burn down their city, let them.

It is not without shame that I type these words; I've come quite a ways since those days. I see such situations in a different light today.

Darin and Dean, however, were more interested. To them, it was an all-day drama with sirens, guns, police cars, fire trucks, smoke, helicopters, and the like. Not realizing that a diet of violence was going to affect them, I took advantage of their gravitating toward the TV each morning. I said things like "Boys, Mommy's going to go clean the bedroom. I want you to call me if the riots are over and Mommy's programs come back on." I left them posted there to make sure I wouldn't miss anything if the riots ended.

I didn't connect some new behavior problems with their television viewing for several days. My children began to act differently. They both seemed more irritable and picky during the day, disagreeing with just about everything one could disagree with. One of them was having difficulty sleeping at night and would wake up screaming. Oh, did that infuriate me! He'd call me and call me until I went to him. I remember many a night when I'd refuse to go right away, but then I worried that my husband wouldn't get enough sleep so eventually I would have to do something. Some nights when I felt particularly tired, I would yell, "Shut up and go to sleep!" If he continued for a while I would go in and paddle him and say, "There's nothing wrong with you. Now you be quiet!" (That's a pretty ridiculous thing to say to someone who's crying hysterically.) Since Dan had to get up early, his patience was wearing thin. Since I love to sleep, I was outraged.

On one night I went into my screaming son's room, jerked him out of bed, and went into the living room where I intended to "have it out" with him. I sat down in a rocker with him on my lap. Because of my anger and frustration I didn't talk, I just rocked. After a while this little boy said in a shaky little voice, "Mommy, I'm so scared. I'm so scared." That was a surprise to me. What did my kids have to be afraid of? So I said, "What are you afraid of? What could possibly hurt you? Mommy and Daddy are here"—which probably wasn't much comfort after the way I'd just yanked him out of bed. "The fire, the fire, is it going to get us? Is it, Mom, is it, Mom?"

I began to say all the things that might appease a little boy. I told him that those fires were way far away from us (I practically pushed Watts around the globe to Viet Nam) and that certainly the police and firemen could handle it (I wanted him to think that the "good guys" always win in the end). I told him that his daddy was strong and that he could ward off all the evils that might befall us. (That is, if the evils came at times he didn't need his sleep). Soon my child fell asleep in my arms. I had successfully convinced him.

I gazed at his angelic face in the moonlight. There was only one problem. I hadn't convinced myself.

It was a long sleepless night for me as I wrestled with fear and uncertainty. How did I *know* it wasn't going to get us? How did I know that it wasn't going to keep spreading right out to our neighborhood? I had heard threats by black people in Watts (on TV) that they just might come out to suburbia and light a few fires. How did I know whether or not they were serious?

I felt upset and it seemed to be coming at the wrong time in my life. I already had problems. I was already feeling mixed-up about life, and I wasn't sure what I was "supposed" to be doing. I was angry at my prayer group for not helping me, or even offering to help me *do* something. My stomach had a knot in it for the next few days.

CHAPTER 2

Monday came and I found myself back in my prayer group. The topic of the day was an upcoming retreat with our associate minister, who'd promised to teach us to pray. How boring it sounded. Why would anyone want to go to "church" for forty-eight hours? I had never been on a retreat before, but it sounded to me like listening to an eight-hour sermon and then getting out our books and talking some more. Talking. I was sick of talking. Then the minister came into our meeting and told us what the retreat would be like—as nearly as he could predict a Spirit-led experience. He said he would answer any questions we had about anything that was important to us and that there would be time spent in prayer. They were actually going to *do* it. Not just talk about it, but *do* it.

Something stirred inside me and I knew I had to go. How would I tell Dan? Was this a good time to leave the children? I had never left my family before. I signed up (probably the first time I ever responded to an inner prompting). I made arrangements for my family and hoped God would take care of them while I was gone. I packed my warm mountain clothes and sleeping bag and left the following Friday for an experience that was to be the foundation for changing the course of my life.

The retreat was exciting from the moment we arrived at

that lovely mountain cabin. There were twelve of us and everyone seemed eager to begin our discussions about prayer. I entered into it wholeheartedly because I was trusting the minister to lead us into the application of what he was teaching, as he'd said he would.

Everyone stayed up late Saturday night and Rev. Stewart led us in a worship time when he invited us to ask Christ into our lives (if we hadn't) or to rededicate ourselves if we'd slipped away. The mood seemed very sacred and I was feeling closer to God than I'd felt for a long time. There was a lot of silence that, for the first time, felt comfortable to me. It was like a dream. He invited us to pray and I remember a wave of fear sweeping over me. I'd never prayed out loud. If I was honest, I wasn't sure I'd ever prayed silently.

All of a sudden, out of the stillness, one of the women stood up and in a loud voice said, "Lord Jesus, I give my life to you. Use me in any way that is your will. Amen." She sat down. I felt a strange jealousy that she did it before I thought of it. It occurred to me that I could do it too. My head got into an argument with my heart at the thought. People will think you're copying (how crazy). God will think you're copying (now that's *really* crazy). Everyone will open their eyes and look at you (the way *I* had when she stood up). Someone will snicker (like my classmates had once in fourth grade when I said I had made up a game). Then the most frightening thought of all: God might take me seriously. Was I ready for that?

While my head and heart had this dialogue, my body (which seems to have a mind of its own) turned to stone. I felt like a statue. I couldn't move. My mouth felt welded shut. My ears were still working though, because I heard the minister say "Amen" and everyone proceeded to get up and make their way to bed. I sat there wanting to yell, "Hey, wait for me! Rewind this film! I was just getting ready to say something or *do* something!" I felt sick. I felt left out. I'd missed my chance to do the very thing that I'd complained about their *not* doing.

Laughter and chitchat from the bunks in the bedroom annoyed me as I sat staring at the fire in the big stone fireplace. I hoped that no one would notice the tears in my eyes. How could I ever go in that room with them? They were acting like kids who'd just been given free passes to Disneyland. How repulsive.

That night I looked for a quiet corner to curl up in, which I found in a room lined with bookshelves. Of all places, a library. Books. I didn't like books. In fact there were times in my life when I hated books. I had never been a reader.

As I found a place for my sleeping bag, I flashed back to my childhood and briefly reexperienced some of the painful times connected with reading. I had been a poor reader. Oh, I sounded good, I could pronounce the words, so the teachers often asked me to read aloud. But what no one seemed to understand was—it didn't stay in my mind. The minute I said the words they were gone. I used to feel so frustrated when I would read a whole page of history, close the book, and not remember what country we were studying. I have a lot of memories of being told that I just wasn't trying or I was lazy. I got the impression that I wasn't very bright and I hated myself for not being able to retain things. I used to cry in my frustration and wonder why academic concepts seemed to fall out of my head.

By sixth grade I had developed a real hatred for reading, a hatred for books and for anyone who enjoyed reading them. I couldn't imagine anyone getting anything out of a book, so if one of my friends said they'd rather read than do something with me, what I heard was that they didn't want to be with me. I must be pretty bad if someone would rather stare at black scratchings on a paper than be with me. Somehow I got through school with passing grades (thank goodness for extra-credit work and salt maps). In my thirty years, I don't think I had ever read a book all the way through. But there I was, choosing to be surrounded with books rather than with those disgustingly happy women.

It became very quiet as the others eventually fell asleep. I lay awake for a long time. I wanted to talk to God but I wasn't sure I knew how to "get through." I'd been groping at learning how to pray but was never sure of when to say

"Thee" and "Thou" and that sort of thing. This was before the new versions of the Bible were popular, so most of us had the King James Version. I had never said a prayer out loud before because I was afraid of making a mistake. If only I could get the prayer I felt in my heart up and out of my mouth, or at least clear in my mind.

Slowly the words began to form and I whispered my first real prayer. "O Lord, I don't know what I'm supposed to be doing with my life. I'm beginning to suspect that you had a reason for creating me at this time in history and in my particular situation. But what is it, Lord? If there's something you want me to be doing, how will I know what the something is? How do you speak to people, Lord?"

My mind flashed to my prayer group and how some of the women would arrive some mornings and say, "The Lord spoke to me last night," or "I talked it over with Jesus and he said . . ." I would become irritated and sort of tune out whatever they said, while saying in my mind, "I bet they're just saying that. Why would God speak to her?" I felt like saying, "Oh, he did not!" I was jealous of their relationship with him. I couldn't stand to think that he talked to them and he didn't talk to me. If he really did talk to them, did that mean he loved them more than me? I shook my head in order to quit thinking about it and went back to my faltering prayer. "Father, how do you talk to your children? How do you communicate, Lord? How would I know if you wanted something of me?"

I don't remember if I was talking aloud or in my mind but I know that I poured out many questions that night without knowing if anyone was really listening. The moonlight caused the room almost to glow and I looked at the thousands of books lining the walls. Titles or authors meant nothing to me, they simply created a colorful design that my eyes enjoyed scanning for a few moments. At some point, my eyes stopped. I wondered why that little blue book looked out of place where it was. All the other books were arranged in graduated sizes, except for one that was wedged between two big volumes of something. Thinking back, I wonder why I even noticed it—there must have been hundreds of blue books. I felt drawn to get up and go over and look at it, and for once I didn't talk myself out of it. That may have been the first miracle in my life. I quietly crawled out of my sleeping bag, went directly to the little book, pulled it off the shelf, and let it fall open somewhere in the middle. The words on the page were distinct in the moonlight. As I read I felt a gentle surge of electricity flow through my body. The words went deep into my soul.

My child, you have been going from person to person seeking Me. Now seek the Light instead of the lamp! I am the Way, the Truth, the Life.

My heart almost stopped. Those words went to my very core. I closed the little book, looked up, and said aloud, "O God, you're here." Again I opened the book.

I want my children to hear My words above all others. You find it hard to believe that I can speak directly to you today. I speak to many who do not hear—who do not want to hear. I tell you, by greatly desiring, by singleness of purpose, by purity of heart, you can hear My words."

God was talking to me. Many questions started spinning in my mind. How was this happening? Who put this book here? Was it just for me? What if I wouldn't have chosen this room? Should I open the book a third time? Certainly *all* the pages wouldn't apply to me. It was probably a coincidence. I slowly opened it again.

I call you to a life of joy, the joy that the mountains at sunset, the birds in the lofty pines, know and express.

That did it. Why would it mention mountains and pine trees? My eyes turned toward the window with the moonbeam shining in. I could see the big pines just outside, and yes, I heard a bird.

Joy flooded through me as I returned to my bed. My mind was clear. I felt loved in a new way. I wanted to sing. Instead, I said very quietly, "Lord, you are here, aren't you! You do hear me when I call, don't you! I love you, Lord. I want to do your will. *Do it*, Lord, not just talk about it. Please guide me in the coming days. O Jesus, will you walk with me? and teach me? I give you my life, Lord, and tomorrow, I'm reporting for duty!" I went to sleep feeling like a child with a secret.

Since that time, many people have heard me tell about that book and they want to know the title and author, as though they think (as I did for a long time) that the book has a special "magic" to it. I've come to believe, as I grow in the knowledge and experience of God through Christ, that the little blue book was not that different from many other beautiful Spirit-filled books available. But I was open in a way I'd never been open before. I had a hunger I'd not experienced before. So I could hear. I believe now that God is always talking to us. He never stops, but our hearing him has to do with our willingness to listen to him, perhaps in some new ways.

CHAPTER 3

I was awakened by the morning sun warming me. The songs of birds reminded me of my promise and of God's promise to speak to me. I could hardly wait to get up and begin my new adventure, but something told me to linger a while and pray that I would be receptive.

I felt prompted to open the book again. It had lain on my pillow all night. This time it said,

To my children I speak in many ways; through My words recorded in the Bible; through the words of My saints of every land, of every century; through sudden convictions in the hearts of those who follow Me. Listen . . . listen. This is the dawn of a new day. Listen for My Will. Desire only My Will.

"O Father," I prayed, "I will try to hear you today in all of the events, in all of my dealings, in what I read and hear others say, in the wind and clouds and trees. O God, help me to listen with new ears. And help me to heed what I hear."

The smell of coffee and the lighthearted chattering in the kitchen eventually lured me out of bed to join the other women. I was startled at how beautiful they looked. My heart felt warm when I realized how very much they each meant to me. The embraces seemed genuine and there was much eagerness to begin the new day. That day I wasn't as interested in talking as in listening. And looking. How lovely things seemed. I wondered how everything could have changed overnight.

The retreat ended at noon with a communion service. During it, I reminded God that I had given my life to him and that as soon as I got home I would be looking for clues as to what he wanted me to do. For the first time I felt as though I understood communion. I accepted by faith that I was forgiven and that through the body and blood of our Lord Jesus Christ I was a new creature. I believed it. Now I had to *be* it and *live* it.

The drive down the mountain with five women talking at the same time, as though they had to get everything said before they got home, found me silently reliving my experience with God the night before. I wanted to savor it. I wondered if I should tell the others about it. Instead I just monitored the questions that began to bubble up in my mind. Will God really speak to me? Will I recognize his voice?

His voice! Why had I always imagined he would sound like a *man*? Will he speak English? I realized I had really limited God up till now. I recalled one time when I raced home from prayer group after one of the members told about God speaking to her. I ran into my bedroom and said, "OK, God. If you spoke to her, why don't you speak to me?" I waited and waited and nothing happened. I guess the only thing I would have settled for was a man's voice. In English.

What will God want me to do? Will Dan mind? Will he even understand?

The next thing I knew, the car was pulling into my driveway and my boys and husband were coming out to greet me. "Did you have a good time?" "Was there any snow?" "Was the food good?" "Did you miss us?" "Hurry up and get ready."

Get ready? For what? Oh, no! How could I have forgotten! If I have to go to that potluck supper I'm going to lose this wonderful spiritual feeling.

Then I remembered. We were in charge of it. Grudgingly I threw together a casserole while Dan helped the boys get ready. Under my breath I told God that he'd have to wait until this was over before I could listen to him. I was sure he didn't attend potluck suppers. Five minutes before we went out the door the phone rang and we found out that the speaker who had been invited wouldn't be there. Now what, I wondered. I hope they don't expect *me* to entertain them. In the mood I was in I'd have probably told them to go back home because they were ruining my retreat experience.

When we arrived at the church we heard that a replacement speaker was on the way. No one knew anything about him, who he was or where he was from—let alone, what he would talk about.

As we were finishing eating our seven kinds of baked beans, four noodle casseroles, and glazed donuts, in the door walked a young man dressed in black with a clerical collar. He had a slide projector and screen and I thought, "Oh, good! It will be dark. I can just sit with my eyes closed and pretend I'm alone. Maybe I'll watch a few slides, maybe not."

The young man was introduced. He was the Rev. Mr. Cooper from a church in the heart of Los Angeles. A ghetto. A slum. A neighborhood so crowded that there's hardly room to breathe. He told about his parish: the 10,000 people living in the shadow of the tall, impressive, downtown office buildings. His church had no congregation—everyone had moved away. He wanted to take us on a trip there via his slide projector.

I found myself interested enough to keep my eyes open. The room was darkened and everyone's attention was fixed on the large screen on stage. We saw where the people lived: shacks, dilapidated hotels, old rundown houses, broken-down cars, alleyways. How can people live like that? Why doesn't somebody *do* something about it?

Faces. Faces. Faces always get me. Mr. Cooper began to introduce us to some of his friends in the inner city. There was Marcy, the daughter of a prostitute, and Barbara, the mother of eight children. There was Arnold, the alcoholic, who slept in the alley, and Marcus, who wanted to learn to read. On and on went the parade of people with problems beyond what my mind could comprehend. Yet, I was engrossed in their stories.

Mr. Cooper told about each person in such a way that I felt I knew them. He really loved those people. He really cared what happened to them. I wondered if he *had* to work there or if he chose to.

Maybe it was the story of the old woman whose two sons had been shot in the riots that brought tears to my eyes, I don't know. It could have been seeing the little children loitering on the church steps looking so forlorn. Something was causing a deep sadness to well up inside me. The speaker's voice faded in and out as I searched for a Kleenex, pretending I was blowing my nose.

Suddenly I became aware of my heart pounding in my chest. I began to feel warm. Uncomfortable. A thought pierced my mind. What if God asked me to go to a place like that? The thought made my heart beat even faster. I was gripping the chair. My knuckles felt numb.

I looked around the darkened room and got the impression that everyone was waiting for a commercial. At least they were looking at the screen and not at me. The thought returned. What if God called me to service in that place? Would I go? Could I go? I began to argue with God in my mind. "Lord, you'd never expect me to go to a ghetto, would you? You know my little kids need me at home. And you know, Lord, how Dan doesn't like for me to be gone very much. Lord, you wouldn't expect me to do something I don't know how to do, would you? And so far from home. Lord, I've never even driven on the freeway by myself! You wouldn't, would you, Lord? Lord?"

In that moment a strange feeling swept over me. I realized that maybe he would. I fell limp in my seat.

Oh, no. Oh, no. Now, what was I going to do? Was this really God? I thought he didn't attend potlucks. Why did I come here anyway?

Again I glanced around the shadows and studied the faces of many of my dearest church friends. Why aren't *they* gripping their seat? Squirming? Why just me?

During the rest of the slide presentation I built a good case in my mind against going by reminding God that I had no education to train me for such work. I wasn't a teacher, nurse, psychologist, social worker, or the like. What could an ordinary housewife from Garden Grove do? I'm a nobody! I can't do anything!

The lights. They seemed so bright. I wanted to get up and run, but Mr. Cooper had a few closing remarks. "I suppose some of you are wondering what you might do to help. You're probably saying to yourself. 'I'm not a professional, I have no credentials, so what can I do?' Well, let me tell you what I *really* need." I couldn't believe it. He was reading my mind. No fair! "What I really need," he said, "is someone who is willing to come to my neighborhood and listen to people. They need to be listened to. They need to know that someone cares. I'm praying that God will send someone to us."

He had just destroyed my argument. I wanted to get out of there. Maybe I need sleep. I've been up a long time.

As I stood up to go for my empty casserole dish, for a moment I had the fear that this was somehow rigged, that Mr. Cooper would see me and say, "There she is. She's the one." Pardon me. Excuse me. I worked my way through the crowd and hurried to the car.

An hour later I was curled up in bed with a pillow over my head, not knowing what kind of night was in store for me. I tossed and turned. Could it possibly have been God? Here I was, twenty-four hours after I'd given my life to him and asked him to guide me, and now I didn't want to believe that he'd really do it. I thought of how critical I'd been of my prayer group members for not doing anything. Wow, I'm glad I didn't tell them about my promise to God. I'd never live it down. I prayed myself to sleep. "Dear God, you know me and my situation here. Do you really want me to leave this and go to help those people? O God, I'm scared! Is it OK to be scared, Lord? I feel so inadequate, so out of it. You know, Lord, how much I love my kids and how much they seem to need me."

At that point I just lay there and watched scenes in my mind. It was as though God said to me, "Fear not, my child, for I am with you and will go before you. It is *because* you love your children that I call you to care about the world they will grow up in." Of course. I *must* be thinking about the world my sons will inherit. Why had I not thought of that before? My awareness had never gone beyond our four walls until this week, and now God wants me to stretch.

"OK, Lord, I'll try. I want to trust you with my life. Thank you for speaking to me. I will try to be obedient." I slept.

CHAPTER 4

The next day was Monday, the beginning of a new week and also the day my prayer group met. I must tell them what is happening inside me. I hope they'll understand.

Before the group began I asked if I could share something. A hush fell over them as I told first about my encounter with God on the retreat and then about my feeling of being led to work in the ghetto. They listened and *heard*.

Several of them encouraged me to go, even if it was just for a visit. Why hadn't I thought of that? A visit.

"Hey," I said, "why don't we all go? It could be like a field trip. We could take canned goods and clothes to donate to the church where Mr. Cooper works." Everyone seemed enthusiastic. (I *knew* sooner or later I'd get them to do a project!)

Within a few days things were arranged and six of us, with assorted children, drove north on the Santa Ana Freeway to a place we'd never been. Because I had a station wagon, I drove. I wasn't sure whether or not to tell them I'd never driven on the freeway before (my husband was always willing to do it). As it ended up, they wouldn't have heard me anyway—with the kids laughing and wiggling and the women seemingly all talking at once.

As we reached the halfway point between Garden Grove

and Los Angeles, my anxiety level began to rise. I became aware of a strange phenomenon taking place inside me. It was as though I was divided into three parts and they were all arguing, all talking at the same time. I tried to sort out what I was feeling and somehow inwardly hearing.

My *heart* seemed to be saying, Yes, yes, this is right. Trust it. Every feeling inside me seemed to be chanting, Go, go, go! I imagined that God was saying, "Finally, you are listening to me." I felt adventurous, courageous. So courageous that I pushed down on the accelerator and noticed that my leg was shaking. Somebody said, "What's wrong with the car? It's kind of thumping." I tuned into my body and began to get a very different message than the one I'd just gotten from my heart. My legs were trembling, my knees shaking. My foot was uncontrollable on the gas pedal. I was perspiring and my head was throbbing. My clammy hands felt slippery on the steering wheel.

I knew that if my *body* could have talked in that moment it would have shouted, "Go back home where it's safe! Go someplace and hide. Relax. Be comfortable!" Which part should I listen to? My feelings or my body? There seemed to be such a contradiction in me.

While I was trying to decide, a third voice rose from within me to be heard. My *mind* had a message all its own. The second I tuned into it I heard, "Boy, is this stupid! You're just going to get yourself killed! Oh, are you ever dumb to think you could do anything to help! What will the neighbors think? What will Dan think?"

Dan. I saw a mental picture of him coming home from work and finding the note I left. "Honey, I've gone to the ghetto to see what I can do." Oh, dear. Why did I leave a note like that? He'll probably faint. I *am* dumb. I *am* stupid. O God, help me to get home before he does. Help! There's a war going on inside me! A riot has broken out! Help!

Which should I listen to? My heart that said Go, or my body that says No, or my mind that says Stupid? I felt so fragmented it was all I could do just to keep driving, hoping someone would tell me when to turn off.

"There's a familiar street," someone in the back seat said. We'd heard Mr. Cooper mention it. I was so eager to get off the freeway that I cut across two lanes of traffic without even looking and decided to trust that our destination was nearby. (Thank you, Lord, for that demonstration of your divine protection.)

What a different world. I found it hard to believe. I had never thought of people living under the freeway off-ramps and overpasses. How many times Dan and I had gone to L.A. to the museum or Farmers' Market on the same freeway. To think there are people living in a slum down under and out of view.

I drove slowly so we could look at the surroundings. Would we find the old church building we'd seen in the slides? I felt strange, looking at people—as if I was invading their privacy. But they got even with us, because they looked at us too.

Someone suggested that we park and walk around. Had they gone mad? Get out? Here? What if someone asks us who we are? Or why we're here? What would we say? (Oh, dear God, what are we doing here?)

We parked. Now what? Everybody's looking at us. Should we get out while they're looking at us? Was I the only one who was afraid? The children were singing, "This old man, he played one." The women were commenting on the style of an apartment building. The next thing I knew, someone was telling the kids we were going for a walk. I was to discover another part of myself in a few moments.

But first, a brainstorm. I had a great idea. "Listen, everybody. When we get out, I think we should act like we know where we're going so the neighborhood people won't think we're just snooping around. Here's my plan. Let's walk down to that corner very confidently, as if we have business here. When we get to the light we turn the corner so the people along here can't see us. We walk very confidently along that street to the next corner and turn, so those people think we know what we're doing. We do it for two more blocks until we get back to our car. How's

that?" I was pleased how well I controlled my voice. I
sounded as cool as a cucumber. I got up on my knees in
the front seat so I could be heard way in the back of the
station wagon. "Kids," I said. "We're going to get out here
and go for a little walk."

They all started yelling things like "I don't want to" and
"Why?" and "I have to go to the bathroom" and "When
are we going to eat?"

I screamed at them and said, "You kids shut up! You get
out there and stand in line. Don't you talk or ask any more
questions." My face felt hot. "Now don't you run ahead
and don't you lag behind and don't you talk to strangers.
Just shut up and do as I tell you!" Where did that come
from? Did that really come out of me? Judging from the
looks on their faces (the kids and the mothers), it must
have. Everyone was in shock. I felt humiliated.

Nevertheless, it worked. The children got out of the car.
They stood in a straight line and there wasn't a sound.
While the women debated whether to take sweaters and
the kids decided to get apples out of their lunch sacks, I
said a quick prayer. "Now God, I've come this far and it
hasn't been easy. We're going to take this walk, so you
have exactly four blocks to tell me what I'm doing here. If
we get back to this car and I haven't heard from you, I'm
going to go home and never come back. You hear that,
God?" I still couldn't believe he was aware of all this.

After the hassle of getting nine people out of the car,
throwing stuff back in, somebody forgetting something,
and so on, we finally slammed the doors and started
walking. We did great for the first fifteen steps and then
one of the mothers said, "By the way, I locked all the
doors so no one would steal anything."

When I heard the word *lock* I froze in my tracks. A
wave of fear swept through me as I turned and announced
that I had left the keys on the floor of the car. Our mission
of mercy was immediately abandoned. We raced back to
the car and proceeded to try to break in with nail files and
bobby pins.

I felt like Job in the Bible when he said, "And the thing
I feared came upon me." A crowd gathered. Every two

minutes someone was asking the two questions I couldn't answer: "Who are you?" "What are you doing here?" I wanted to scream, "How would I know!" Instead I concentrated on my amateur lock-picking skills until the police came. Honestly, officer, it's *our* car. For a person who didn't want to be stared at, breaking into a car was not a very cool thing to do.

My body temperature was rising as the police called the neighborhood fire department to help them break in to get the keys and check the registration. As the crowd grew in size I found myself hiding in the shadows under the archway of a building. Where was God?

Soon the firemen opened the door, then all four doors. The crowd applauded. We said, "Oh, we don't want to get in, officer." Most of the crowd shrugged their shoulders, shook their heads, and walked away. But the neighborhood children stayed on for awhile. Our kids started saying, "Hi" and they answered back. A few women stood nearby as though they were keeping an eye on their children until these strangers moved on.

I could understand their concern so I walked over to them and said in a calm voice, "We don't know why we're here. We aren't anyone special, but we live in a different town and we wanted to visit your neighborhood and get acquainted with some of you." That was neat. Completely honest. Why hadn't I thought of that sooner? I went on to say that we hoped to learn about their community and that with their permission we'd like to visit them every week and get to know them better.

I couldn't believe what I was hearing myself say. I had thought we were there to try to "help" these people and there I was saying we'd come to learn from them. I don't know how that came out of my mouth because I'd never thought of it before. It made me think that perhaps God was involved in this after all.

I imagined they would be excited that these neat-looking mothers with pretty children had come all this way to get acquainted with them. Shock. They just stared at us.

"Can you tell us about your neighborhood? Or can we walk around and look at it?" we asked.

"Yeah, go ahead."

So we wandered around for awhile with the neighborhood children following us (to our children's delight). Eventually we found the old church we'd seen in the slides.

I experienced my second shock when the minister didn't seem overly enthralled either. We found him up to his neck in rummage in the church basement. Signs out in front announced a Giant Rummage Sale. After we got his attention, we said "Hello! Here we are! We came to help the people in the ghetto."

His blank stare made me realize he'd probably shown his slides to hundreds of groups, so why did I expect him to say, "Oh, you're the people from Garden Grove"?

What could we do? Somehow his telling us we could sort rummage didn't set right. "We mean, out in the community. We want to help with those kinds of things."

Whoever would have thought we'd be spending the day going door to door in 100-degree heat, inviting people to a rummage sale? Inside, I felt let down. I thought he would welcome us with open arms, maybe even cry. I wanted him to fall on his knees and say, "Thank you, God, for sending these friends here." Oh, well. This door-knocking wasn't what I had in mind as a new career either. In the weeks to come, I was to learn many things about myself.

I felt hollow as I fearfully knocked on each door. This neighborhood was made up of many different ethnic groups—Mexican, Oriental, Black, Italian, German, etc. Some people were suspicious. Some were friendly. Some just closed the door. Some said, "Thank you."

As I reflect on those early inner-city experiences I am amazed at how I can now see God's hand moving in my life. While I was *living* it, though, I constantly questioned his whereabouts.

I marvel at his timing. Although I don't suppose he staged the Watts riots for my thirtieth birthday, I do believe that he guided my every step from the moment of my commitment.

Thank you, Lord, for teaching me.

CHAPTER 5

A new era opened in my life. That trip was the first of many we were to make to that inner-city community and to the Rev. Mr. Cooper's church. It was never again as difficult as it was the first time.

Sometimes I would drive to the old church and sit on the front steps with my guitar and sing with the neighborhood children. It gave me the feeling I had something to give that they would receive. We didn't see much of Mr. Cooper, since he spent most of his time out in the parish as a sort of troubleshooter.

Yet we began to make friends we could talk to. With a sense of wide-eyed wonder, I visited the women we met on that first day. I spent time in their apartments, watching their children play. I listened to despair and frustration as it seeped out through the small talk. They became my teachers, and I learned many things.

I met mothers who knew nothing about child care—or about child prevention, since this was before the days of free birth-control advice. I held babies who had diaper rash from their toes to their noses because their mothers didn't know what to do about it. I watched two-year-olds being given a bottle of curdled milk since the family didn't have a refrigerator. The bigger kids got whatever food there was. I saw scurrying cockroaches. I heard children crying hour after hour for no outwardly evident reason. I was excited at the thought that perhaps I could help them with some of these problems. I had a background of Dr. Spock, *Parents' Magazine*, TV, and a mother who seemed to know all sorts of inexpensive home remedies.

Many women in that neighborhood couldn't even tell time. Shock. None had watches. Few had clocks in their apartments. That discovery was made after I had excitedly arranged for several of them to get together to learn more about child care. They seemed eager when we planned it, but when I showed up at the empty church on Wednesday morning at ten, the time agreed upon, no one was there. I began to wonder if I hadn't misread them. I went around to their apartments and asked why they hadn't come to the church. The answer they all gave was the same. They didn't know what time it was. How can someone *not* know what time it is? That, however, was not as startling as discovering that many of them also did not know what month or day it was. Those factors made it very hard to plan anything. At first it seemed to me that they were not dependable. If I drove forty-five miles on a Wednesday and arrived at such and such a time, I expected them to be there and act appreciative.

Finally I felt comfortable enough with Barbara to ask why she wasn't more interested in knowing the time, or what day it was, or the date. It simply didn't matter, she explained. For her, every day was the same. Nothing happened, she had no place to go, no one came, she had nothing to do. Besides, what difference did anything make?

"Barbara," I said, "you must have something in your life that you don't want to miss. Isn't there something you look forward to?"

Her answer haunted me for days: "Yeah, I look forward to dying."

How could it be? Someone the same age as I. All of a sudden I had all these things to live for. How could a life be so empty? "O Lord, help me to help Barbara find a reason to go on living. A reason, Lord. Something exciting."

In the days to come I found many things I could do. For example, I learned that the women were consistently being shortchanged by the traveling bread vendors who honked their horns every morning looking for customers. I found that if I just went out to the curb and stood there with the person, the man's ability to do math seemed to improve.

It's strange how before I went to the inner city I used to think, "But what can I do? I don't know anything about their problems. There's no way I could help!" How different it is after you arrive. The question "What can I do?" never comes up. If you see a mother with five kids pushing a grocery cart six blocks home from the store, you simply help her or pick up one of the kids. If you see a blind man afraid to cross the busy street, you take his arm and lead him across. If a child is lost, you take her door to door until you find where she belongs. If someone is sick and he has no phone to call a doctor, you find out where one is and take him there. It seemed so simple once I was actually doing it. So natural. And no one asked to see my credentials.

As I learned more about the problems the people had, such as not being able to read well, I began to feel some old fears creep in. I prayed, "Lord, these people need to learn. They need to know what day it is and what time it is. They need to learn to read a calendar and to make change. Lord, they need to learn to read so they can get jobs and read labels in the supermarket and read instructions on medicine bottles. I know, Lord, that I can help them with some of the stuff, but the reading—you *know* that reading has never been my thing. Right? Please, Father, send someone to your children here who can teach them to read and write. Thank you, Father. Amen."

It was amazing how my prayer life was changing. I seemed to be having this constant dialogue with God. I *did* seem to be doing most of the talking, but I knew he was listening. I could see many signs of his working.

Life had become an adventure. I never knew from one minute to the next what I'd be doing.

Not long after that I was introduced to a woman named Helen Line. She was the most radiant, spiritual person I'd

ever met. I wanted to be around her, and I found myself
inquiring about who she was and what she did. I got goose
bumps when she told me that she taught Laubach Literacy
Teacher Training. It was a method of teaching adults to
read and write in a very short time—or to speak English if
they didn't know how. I was stunned. I'd never heard of
Frank Laubach, the incredible man who spent years helping people all around the world learn to read and write.

She told about the groups of people she'd trained to
establish literacy centers where adults could learn in an
atmosphere of love and encouragement. It sounded so
beautiful. Did we dare to ask her to teach us? Was this
God's answer to our need, so that *we* could become teachers to those who seemed to need it desperately?

One of my friends asked her sort of jokingly, "You
wouldn't want to drive 100 miles to Los Angeles to teach a
class, would you?" Her response was, "Oh, I've been
wanting to do that. I'd love to!"

Within a few weeks a literacy class was started for
would-be teachers each to become a tutor, since the Laubach method advocates a close, caring relationship between teacher and student.

After a few weeks we opened our Literacy Center. I had
a sense of pride in having something more definite to offer
than a love that was clouded by fears and uncertainties.

I'll never forget my first student. I showed up at the
church that day with my workbooks and a bag of objects
that were part of the first reading lesson. I set up a table
with tablet and pencil neatly arranged next to the student's workbook. The other teachers were at their tables
also awaiting their first students. I wondered who I'd get.

One by one people began to arrive in response to the
flyers that were passed out by neighborhood children. One
of my friends was acting as hostess and introducing the
new person to one of the teachers. I watched as each of
my friends were coupled with a student. I was the only
teacher without one.

Finally a woman came through the door—a short,
plump, troubled-looking person of about fifty-eight, whose
drab housedress seemed to match the color of her skin.
"Lord, she's not the one I want! I want someone young!

Lord, they're telling me she doesn't speak any English, only Spanish. Help! I don't know one single word of Spanish! Lord, here she comes. They're bringing her to me. Where are you, Lord?" I wanted to run.

Mrs. Aguilar was introduced to me, and neither of us smiled as she sat down across from me. We stared at each other, not knowing what to do. My eyes pretended to be busy. I gazed at the workbook and my little objects neatly placed there. Somehow they looked dumb: the cracked plastic bird, the cup, the artificial egg. I hoped she wouldn't notice them. How could I start? I had rehearsed how I would begin so many times in the last week, anticipating this moment. Why were things always different than I planned? I couldn't even think of a prayer to pray, except that she would disappear—and I doubted that God would go for that. O God, help me.

I looked around at my friends and their students, some of whom were also Mexican. I heard the soft mumbles and the rustle of pages. I saw a Spanish-English dictionary on a table nearby. As I searched my mind for something to look up, I stepped over and picked it up. I was sure that Mrs. Aguilar could hear my heart pounding from the fear that filled me. A thought flashed through my mind: "Tell her you're afraid." Why would I do a thing like that? Again it came: "Tell her you're afraid." While I was thumbing through the dictionary, my head was saying "How will she ever respect her teacher if she knows she's scared?"

I found the word for "teacher," since my name, Rhea, is not in the dictionary. Then I kept my finger between the pages as I searched for "afraid." OK, Lord, here goes.

My voice quivered as I somehow pronounced those two words. I felt too dumb to look directly at her for what seemed like an eternity. I looked at her hands, twisting each other. My eyes traveled up her dark-skinned arms to her tired-looking shoulders and then to her face. There were tears in her eyes. Her face began to soften. She opened her mouth and, like a waterfall, words came tumbling out. Spanish words.

One of my friends who could speak a little Spanish came over and said, "She's telling you, 'Thank you, thank you,' for saying you're afraid because she is very frightened also. She wants to learn to speak English so much, but she's afraid she's too old. She says she started toward the church three times but didn't have the courage to open the door. The fourth time, she made herself come in. She prayed that God would get her a good teacher and she is now saying, 'Thank you, God.' "

When I heard that, I wanted to cry. We ended up hugging each other while our tears turned to laughter.

We sat back down, took a deep breath, and she wrote her name on her workbook. The lesson was underway.

CHAPTER 6

A beautiful experience resulted from that first teaching experience. Mrs. Aguilar was the manager of an old apartment building across the street. It was a three-story, wooden, condemned disaster with rusted fire escapes hanging on the sides and with windows so dirty one could hardly see through them. I always worried that the sagging balcony would fall on the people who were lying around on the porch below. Within a few months our little group from Garden Grove would be renting an apartment in that firetrap. That way our families could join us on weekends to find out what was going on that had captured all our hearts.

As our teaching and relating continued, there was still a lot of suspicion about our presence in that neighborhood. We were watched through the curtains by many who still wondered just what we were doing there. They were surprised and even more suspicious when we began to move things into the apartment and spend hot summer nights on the porch with them.

There were about thirty rooms in our new "home," each occupied by people of varying backgrounds. None of them associated with the others—that is, until we arrived. In our innocence we held an "open house" after we had fixed up our twelve-by-twelve room with new plastic curtains and assorted chairs. Many of the tenants came to meet us. This had never happened before.

The first weekend we spent there had a profound effect on my family. Dan and I and the boys packed as though we were going camping. We took sleeping bags, easy-to-prepare food, cots, and a suitcase of clothes for each of us. Another suitcase was filled with books and games to entertain us after we were in for the night. We were quite a sight as we carried our gear down the long, dark, dingy corridor to the last room on the left. No one welcomed or even spoke to us as we moved in—although several doors opened a chain's length and eyes could be seen checking us over.

The old creaky door must have had twenty coats of paint on it, judging from the colors showing where it was chipped or peeling. There were six locks on the door, spaced above and below the holes where locks had been broken out. Some had chains, some bolts, hasps, and so on. When we closed the door that first night, my sons made sure the locks were all secured. Then one of them said, "Mommy, did we lock them *out* or lock ourselves *in*?" I really didn't know. I was so frightened about being overnight in this neighborhood, I couldn't even think.

It was a hot summer night. It must have been 114° in that asphalt jungle. But because there was only one window and we were afraid to open it, there was no air to breathe. Actually, the window had been painted shut. Nor did we feel comfortable with the curtains parted, since the window looked out into an alley where there was a lot of nighttime activity—which probably explains why no one ever opened it.

The night that became a nightmare had only just begun. No one wanted to play games. It was too hot and stuffy. We couldn't read. It was too hard to concentrate with noises on all sides that we strained to identify. Why hadn't we brought our portable TV? Oh, yes, we had wanted to "rough it."

About ten P.M., Darin and Dean wanted something to eat. Unfortunately, we found cockroaches in the chocolate chip cookies they had helped make for the occasion. At ten-thirty, an argument broke out in the apartment across the hall. A man and woman were hollering violently, saying things I didn't want my boys to hear. They began to fight and we could hear thumping, screams, and cursing. "Come on, children, let's sing." I said with about as much enthusiasm as a person in a shipwreck. "On top of old Smokey . . . "

"Come on, Dan, you want to sing, don't you?"

It didn't work. "Mommy, what's a son of a _____? What does _____ mean? How come that man is calling that lady a _____?"

On the other side of us a baby cried for hours while a woman's voice yelled and cursed above the screams. We heard loud banging as though she was shoving the crib against the wall to the rhythm of, "You shut up or I'll kill you."

In the apartment above us loud music played until three in the morning. People danced and stomped. The bass notes caused the paint to fall in little flakes from our ceiling. We noticed the ceiling because we didn't turn the light out all night; the room would have been totally black without the one and only bare light bulb swaying from the ceiling.

We heard people shouting out in the hall and chasing each other in the alley. "Lord, what am I supposed to do as a trying-to-be-caring person? I'm afraid to open the door and peek out, let alone interfere." Offering to help, I feared, would be interfering.

"Mommy, I have to go potty." Oh no! You *can't* have to go potty! There was only one potty, a dirty toilet in a closet down the hall, shared by forty people on the floor. In the daylight I had always chosen to walk three blocks to the gas station.

"Children, you'll have to wait until morning," I said, anger creeping into my voice. Their chins began to quiver. "I'm hot! I want to go home! I don't like it here!" they both began to chant. I felt the patience and sanity draining out of me as though someone had pulled a plug.

I faced Dan, whom I had avoided looking at for the last hour as he had paced back and forth across this stuffy little room. Occasionally he changed his gait to step on a bug. He was mumbling. I imagined he was saying, "You and your wild ideas! Why did I ever let you talk me into this?"

Finally, there we were, lying in sleeping bags designed for the Arctic, on camping cots that squeaked with every move. I turned over in my sweaty sleeping bag and felt so angry that I wanted to beat someone up. It was the longest night of my life.

When morning came we were wilted, like flowers in a vase without water. The only reason we made it through the night was that we knew we could go home in the morning if we wanted to. How did those with no way out ever get through it? How did they survive without going stark raving mad? In such conditions, the frustration mounts until every building has sticks of human dynamite with fuses burning. The occupants have nothing to lose by going crazy.

But this was the day for our big surprise. We had brought our electric ice cream freezer and the ingredients for strawberry ice cream. Dean and Darin were all re-hearsed to go up and down the halls and out onto the fire escape to invite all our neighbors to come and join us for giant cones.

It created quite a stir when we blew a fuse in the old building and needed to search the musty basement for the fuse box. The sound of the freezer churning away brought people down the hall to check out what was going on.

That day Dan must have given out forty bright pink ice cream cones to forty eager people. Then we closed up our little room, drove home, and recuperated for two days.

Months went by, yet my friends and I diligently kept returning to the place that had captured our hearts, to the people who were breaking our hearts. We were gaining more and more insight into the problems our inner-city friends face. We knew we couldn't begin to look for solutions until we understood what the problems were. Each of us was being led in a different direction as we got more and more involved with our students and their families. Even as I write this, I'm aware that the women who went with me may not recognize my account of the experiences. I suppose we each saw things from our own perspective and interpreted the events differently— depending on our interests, expectations, understanding, and memory.

I became friends with a young mother who taught me something valuable. Lupe was a challenge at first, not because of her learning ability but because of my not wanting to work very close to her. You see, Lupe had worn the same clothes for four months and her body odor seemed unbearable. I didn't want to offend her or lose her as a student. When truckloads of clothing were delivered to the inner-city church for a rummage sale, compliments of several middle-class suburban churches, I got the idea of taking Lupe as my guest and "treating" her to some pretty new clothes. The big rummage sale was planned for the same day that Lupe and I usually met for our lesson. It seemed natural to say "Hey, Lupe, let's go see what they have at the rummage sale." No response. "Don't you think it's a good idea?"

"I'll go if you want to go," she said, "but I don't need anything."

I was baffled by her lack of interest. I was sure she'd get excited after she saw the neat things I'd noticed on the days I'd helped to sort and price things. But I gave up after asking her six times if she liked something and would like me to buy it for her. Her answers were always "Yes" and "No." Yes, she liked it, and No, she didn't want it.

As we walked back to her apartment, where she spent most of her time with her two babies, I shared my disap- pointment with her. I said I had so hoped to buy her something as a gift. In the cool of the evening she began to share with me something that was to open my eyes to a new level of understanding. This is what she told me.

"I don't need anything. These clothes are all I got, but they're enough. I don't have a washer, or a dryer, or an iron (this was before permapress days). I don't even have a place to hang clothes." Her voice trailed off. There were tears in her eyes. "And besides, why dress up when nobody cares?"

I felt as if I'd been stabbed. I ached to say, "Oh, Lupe, I

do! I care!'' But the words just wouldn't come out of my mouth.

In the coming weeks, however, I became determined to show her how much I cared, and I saw a miracle one day as I sat in the church basement waiting for her. In the door came a lovely young woman in a flowered blouse and neat slacks. I would have sworn it was Lupe. My mind argued and said it can't be. Lupe's hair always looked like an explosion and this person's hair was neatly pulled back and held by a red rubber band. She came over to my table and stood looking at me. My heart skipped a beat.

"Lupe!" I said, trying to control the shock in my voice. "You look beautiful! What's happened to you?" She invited me to my feet by extending her hand and threw her arms around me. "I wanted to dress up for my teacher because I'm so happy! Now somebody cares!" O God, how could I have been a part of such a transformation? Lord, I actually saw her change from a caterpillar to a butterfly right before my eyes. Thank you, Lord, for what you are teaching me through these beautiful people—these hurting, frustrated, lonely, inwardly beautiful people.

I was learning about motivation. If you feel that nobody cares, why get up in the morning? Why clean house? Why dress up? Why work? Why care? Time and time again I saw the miracle that took place when an individual became convinced that someone really cared about him.

CHAPTER 7

I wondered if the people from suburbia who sent their rummage to the ghetto went to bed at night thinking, "Well, I've helped the poor today." What would they do if they found out that a lot of their stuff is still lying there, because the people they wanted to help didn't even have the motivation to dress up or change? The poor need donations of food and clothing, but it takes more than that to make a productive person. I've seen many people eat a big donated meal and get up the next day to the same problems with no hope.

Hope. That's what they need most of all. How can I give these people hope? O Lord, you have become my hope, my *only* hope. Show me how to tell my new friends about you.

Talking to them seemed so strained, because many of the words I used had different meanings to them. In a meditation time one night at home, a realization came to me. Everyone has inside himself a slide tray (the kind you put into a projector) with a slide for each word he knows. When someone says a word to him, the slide pops up and he sees his interpretation of that word. Every person might see a different picture for the same word.

For example if I said the word "home" to someone in the ghetto, the picture that might flash before his inner

eyes might be of a rat-infested, rundown apartment building. Or a room that he shares with nine other people. Yet
in my mind I'm seeing my lovely, landscaped, newly
painted house in Garden Grove. There wouldn't be much
real communication between us.

If I said the word "father," I would be seeing a protec-
tive, industrious head of a household. What would the
other person be seeing?

When you get into words like "love" you really can't
imagine what scene flashes in the person's mind. How
could I ever tell anyone about God? Love? Hope?

Lord, how can I tell them about you, about Love, so
they'll have hope? What, Lord? I must *act* it out! Now wait
a minute. I'm not good at acting. I must *become* those
qualities if I'm to communicate them? Well, help me know
how to do it. Calm the fears that arise within at the very
thought.

I became dedicated to the task of demonstrating my
love, of bringing some hope, to those I met in that inner-
city community. Yet somehow I knew I would eventually
have to talk to the people I lived with in white suburbia.
They needed to know what I was discovering, to help the
situation through many expressions of caring and love. I
knew it would take more money, food, assistance, hours,
legal knowledge, power, and connections.

My crusade to make a difference in the world led me on
to another location after I met a wonderful black man
named Jimmy Brown. He operated a job-placement bureau
in an old abandoned gas station in a community called
Willowbrook. Jimmy contacted me after a story appeared
in the newspaper about our Literacy Center in the church.
He asked if I'd come to his place and open a center where
his friends could learn to read and write. Not having those
skills was keeping many of them from getting jobs.

Once again, I was to have many more experiences to
teach me as I consented to go with him. This new area
seemed so much more hostile than the one downtown.
Willowbrook was much closer to Watts, and the emotional
climate seemed tense and explosive.

No one showed up for my first class. It had been hard to

walk with my satchel of books through crowds of loitering men in front of the old gas station while everyone stared at me. I felt humiliated to walk back through them. A failure. As influential as Mr. Brown was in that community, he was unable to persuade anyone to come in and learn from me. Intellectually I understood it, but inside I felt shattered. I had been so excited and I wanted to help so much. Jimmy wanted me to try again, but I wasn't sure I could risk the embarrassment of carrying my things in and waiting for people who never came.

As I prayed about it, an image came to my mind. I saw a scene of a bunch of black children crowded around me as I played my guitar. If I did that, would the kids walk away? OK, Lord, one more time. I'll go.

The next time I went to Willowbrook, a large truck was parked in front of the gas station with about thirty kids crowded around it. Some organization had donated a truckload of toys to Jimmy Brown. He was tied up on the telephone, but when he saw me he asked me to help sort and distribute the toys. As I did that, he would appear on the scene once in awhile and say, "Now you kids listen to this lady. She's in charge!"

We put the toys in piles: big-boy toys, little-boy toys, big-girl toys, little-girl toys, broken toys. I wouldn't have sorted them the way the children did, especially now with our awareness of sexism, and men's and women's roles having changed so much in recent years. But the children had very definite ideas about boy and girl things.

One stack of toys was much bigger than the others: the broken ones. I couldn't believe how many trucks without wheels, books with torn-out pages, puzzle boxes half full, and games with missing pieces we were finding. I felt embarrassed. I was ashamed that "my kind of people" would think that anyone would want the things they were giving away. Did the donors go to bed that night thinking they'd done a great thing by giving junk their own kids wouldn't play with to the "poor deprived" children in the ghetto? One little boy's face lit up when he reached for a bright yellow Tonka truck. "Hey, this is mine!" Then he discovered that the wheels were missing, and he tossed it.

My "mother-part" automatically shamed him by saying, "Is that any way to treat a gift?" What a *dumb* thing to say! What did I expect? His response was, "Why do people think we want a thing after the play's gone all out of it?"

Eventually I convinced a few of them that it could be fun to repair things by combining parts of several broken toys. We couldn't think of anything to do with the used coloring books, though! Also, I was amazed and angered by the number of guns and war toys my suburban friends had given these children. The kids thought it was great, though, because they could "practice."

I returned to Willowbrook several times that week to help with the toys, and each time I went I was shocked to see toys strewn all over the neighborhood. If they weren't broken when they arrived, they were then. It didn't take long for me to recognize that the children in this ghetto had the same attitude I had found in so many adults. Nothing really matters. The kids couldn't take pride in themselves. And from the way they behaved, the young people I met, the teen-agers didn't seem to think they were anyone important either—or that anyone cared if they lived or died. I began to pray about how I might relate to them.

In a few days I found myself living out my earlier meditation: sitting on the curb in front of the Job Corporation with my guitar and about thirteen youth. It was a start. It was all right for now. But I'd have to do more if I was going to matter to this community. Lord, what can I do that's creative and constructive? What can I share with them that will give them hope? Speak to me, Lord.

One day when I arrived home I received a phone call from a man I'd never met, asking if I had any use for about thirty partial cans of paint. He had completed some project and had heard of my interest in Willowbrook. Without having the slightest idea of what I'd use the paint for, I said, "Sure, I'll take them."

Before they were even delivered, the idea came. I visited lumber companies in my area and asked for donations of scrap wood, and the next time I went to Willowbrook, I had a carload of wood and thirty cans of assorted colors of paint. Little did I know that that was the beginning of the Willowbrook Jig Saw Puzzle Company, owned and operated by the young people who hung around the Job Corporation.

The children were excited to see what I had and immediately began to paint their own creations on the pieces of wood. At the end of the day we had an art exhibit: twenty-five artistic creations leaning against the wall of the old gas station. Many of the paintings were done on square pieces of plywood, about a foot square. A thought flashed into my mind: if I could find a power jigsaw, perhaps the children could learn to cut their pictures into puzzle pieces and we could sell them.

Wow! That seemed exciting, not only to me but to the youngsters. All I had to do was figure out where I could get a jigsaw. The Lord reminded me that the Men's Club at my church was having their monthly meeting the very next day. Dear God, please go with me as I ask them if they'll donate the money for one. I think I'm more scared of them than the people in Willowbrook!

The next time I went to Willowbrook, I had a shiny new deluxe jigsaw in a suitcase. My husband and I had practiced with it the night before so that I could teach them how to use it.

The Jig Saw Puzzle Company officially opened its doors that day. Twenty young people diligently and creatively cut their artistic expressions into puzzle pieces and we began to discuss our "marketing plan." Their suggestion was that they would be glad to paint them and it would be my job to sell them—which didn't seem very fair to me at first. The first summer produced about 300 wooden puzzles, each mounted on a piece of masonite that served as a tray. I had no problem selling them for one dollar each to almost everyone I met in my church, and especially at the next Men's Club meetings. As the word spread, I was delivering barely dry puzzles to kindergarten teachers, nursery schools, and churches, as well as to many of my friends, who gave them as gifts.

The children had to elect a president and a treasurer to

handle the money and help plan how to spend it. It was decided at the end of a long hot summer that it would be spent on field trips. As the children tried to agree on *where*, I worked on the *how*. That first year we visited the Los Angeles Museum, went to an Angels baseball game in Anaheim, made a trip to the beach in Capistrano, as well as attended (with their mothers as their guests) one of the largest and most beautiful churches in Southern California for a luncheon and party. For many of them, it was the first time they had been out of the ghetto. Even more significant, it was the first time some of them had ever felt important or proud or cared-about.

Thank you, God, for the wondrous way you work things out. You seem to have an answer for everything. Help me to remember to ask.

Only once was I afraid during that time. One day we had an unusually large group of young people wanting to paint. As an alternate activity, I had brought a bucket of homemade play-dough for those waiting their turn to paint or saw. I was trying hard to be fair and remember who was next. The door opened and in sauntered two tall, muscular black boys who looked about seventeen. They stood inside the door and just stared at me until a hush came over the room. Who were these fellows? What did they want? Should I say anything?

I felt my face flush as I told the children to ignore them and continue with their particular project. Why were they looking at me like that? Why didn't they say something? I decided to ignore them too, and I began complimenting some of the children on their work. All of a sudden I felt something hit my right shoulder with a sting. Instinctively, I reached across with my left hand to the spot. I felt something wet. Had I been shot? I looked at my hand and saw green paint oozing between my fingers.

Slowly I turned to the big boys who stood across the room from me, still and staring like statues. One of them took some play-dough from the bucket and, without looking down, slowly formed it into a ball. What was he going to do? When he got it rolled about the size of a big marble, he slowly reached over to a paint can and dunked it in, still without taking his eyes off me.

What is this game he's playing, I wondered. My heart began to pound. Another sting, this time on my face. Again my hand went to the place as though it could change the feeling, and I felt sticky orange paint running down my cheek. Lord, I'm scared! Why are they doing this? What should I do?

Two more times I felt the piercing pain and the humiliation of the dough-balls hitting me before I could gather enough courage to react. Suddenly several of the children noticed that their paintings were being damaged by the dripping paint as the wads of dough flew through the air, and they began to holler—*at* me, not at the boys! "Teacher, make 'em quit! Teacher, get 'em out of here! Look at my picture . . . it's ruined! My pretty picture is ruined! Teacher . . ."

I felt rage well up inside me but I was afraid to let it come out. It's one thing if they mess *me* up a little bit, but these kids have been working hard for days on their pictures. It's not fair for these big brutes to destroy their efforts.

I didn't know what to do. I felt anger, fear, humiliation, hurt, the desire to defend being drowned by the desire to run.

Then I did something I still can't believe. I looked one of them right in the eyes as he was sculpting his next bullet. Without bumping into a single table, I walked through the crowd of kids right up to him. In a voice that sounded calm, I said very clearly, "Get out!" Without taking my eyes off his eyes, my hands seemed guided to his and I simply took the dough out of his big hand and placed it in the bucket. With my two hands on his chest I said again very slowly, "I said get out!" (O God, I think I'm going to faint!) He glanced at his buddy, who sort of jerked his head as though to gesture, "Let's go." With no other words and no resistance, the two young men turned toward the door and made their exit.

I closed the door and felt my knees buckle. I sat on the nearest box and felt my body experience all of the feelings that had been under control for that ten-minute drama. I trembled, I was mad, I wanted to cry. I felt raped, mocked. But I was OK. In fact, I'd won! Or is there a winner?

I looked at my blouse with four colors of paint splashed on it. I felt my orange cheek with my green hand. I looked at the kids who'd returned to their work and were chattering as though nothing had happened. I felt sadness inside, perhaps because I wanted everyone to like me and I didn't know how to relate to those boys. Or maybe because the experience had frightened me to the core and might affect my desire to return. Or was it the image of Jesus I saw in my mind, being taunted and provoked, mocked and humiliated? I could almost feel a crown of thorns. Jesus, how did you stand up under that kind of thing? How did you keep on loving them? How could you ever give your life for people like that? And for people like me?

The puzzle company operated for three years. The youngsters discovered the joy of accomplishment and the pleasure of rewards.

CHAPTER 8

Jimmy Brown's wife, Kitty, was expecting a baby, and all of the neighborhood children were excited about it. I asked her one day if she had ever had a baby shower (she had two other children) and she looked at me questioningly. "Does it rain babies?" she asked with a laugh.

"Kitty," I said. "Mark this date on your calendar. I'm going to have a shower for you in my home. People will bring gifts for your baby. It will be great fun."

"But who would ever give me gifts?" she asked shyly. I told her she'd just have to wait and see.

When I got home that evening I began to write out invitations to the women in my church circle and prayer group. How would they feel about coming to a shower for a black woman they'd never met? How would my neighbors react when a black family arrived at my home? I wasn't aware of any black families within eight miles of my house.

I spent all day getting ready for the special event. I bought streamers, balloons, favors, fancy napkins and tablecloth, and a special cake from a local bakery in the shape of a baby's gown, yellow with icing to resemble embroidery and ribbons. I hadn't encouraged RSVPs since it seemed I was rarely home.

The night came and people began to arrive. We waited

for Kitty and Jimmy to find their way through the maze of freeways from their home forty miles away. When they arrived, with daughter Linda, seven years old, there were thirty-two women who could hardly wait to yell, "Surprise!"

What an experience to watch Kitty open gift after gift! She exclaimed again and again that she couldn't believe anyone would give her such lovely things when they didn't even know her. Her eyes were focused in her lap most of the time as she tried to save every piece of wrapping paper and ribbon. As soon as one gift was opened and the group "ooed" and "aahhhed" someone put another one in her lap. I'll never forget her comment as her eyes met ours. "If I wasn't so black, I'd turn red all over!" Everyone roared, jumped up, came to her, and gave her a big hug. It was a moving sight to see such love. There were tears in Kitty's eyes.

There was one traumatic moment that night when we all filed into the kitchen to see the beautiful cake. Kitty kept saying, "Oh my! Oh my!" and it was obvious that she loved it. When she was handed a giant knife, she wasn't able to cut it. Finally someone took the knife, went "whomp," and cut one of the "arms" off the baby gown cake. Kitty burst into tears! She couldn't believe we would destroy that gorgeous cake.

After several cameras recorded the scene, we persuaded her to let us divide the cake into thirty-some pieces. It was a night to remember.

I was reminded of it several times by neighbors who had panicked when they saw blacks going into our house. We even received a letter warning us not to consider selling our house to blacks or there would be trouble.

After two and a half years of involvement in the inner-city church and in Willowbrook I began to get tired. Weary was really the word. The fact that everything looked the same and the problems still remained (unemployment, unwanted babies, despair, violence, poverty) made me wonder if I was accomplishing anything. Was I doing this work just to salve my conscience? It didn't seem that I was making a difference.

And my home life was beginning to show signs of gross neglect. My family didn't want to hear my stories anymore. I began to feel martyred and alone. Lord, what is this feeling? Are you calling me to leave the city? Or am I giving up? I really don't know. Lord, I had thought you led me to this place.

In time, I was to learn that God leads me *to* something or someone, not necessarily to stay there all my life, but to go *through* it, learning the lessons it has for me. I sometimes have trouble remembering to ask God if and when he wants me to quit something and move on. Ruts are sort of secure.

During this time of questioning, I received an invitation to speak to a PTA group at a nearby school. At first that seemed more frightening than working in the ghetto. Then I realized that when I was working with people in the ghetto, there was great need. I often knew things they didn't know simply because of my upbringing. But it was a different story in my own community. I'd always felt inadequate because I hadn't gone on to school. I felt dumb and out of it around educated people. I'd never thought of myself as attractive and I didn't wear clothes with impressive labels. My nervousness was caused by the fear that the other women would talk about me or not like me. Or that I'd say something using poor grammar and people would laugh (or worse, look disgusted). Lord, are you in this?

I needed to mull the possibility over in my mind for a couple of days before I could give an answer. During that time, I was reminded of my prayer of commitment to God, that I'd go anywhere he wanted me to go. In fact, I'd even hoped he'd find something in Garden Grove. Why did God always seem to surprise me? OK, Lord, I'll accept.

I called the PTA president, who immediately set up a date with a newspaper photographer and told me that flyers would be sent home with every child. They anticipated a large crowd since many people were interested in race relations at that time.

In a few weeks I made my debut as a public speaker. I had taken slides of some of my inner-city friends, their houses, the abandoned church, etc., and had decided to give a simple talk about how the situation looked through the eyes of an untrained, unskilled, unknowledgeable, scared housewife. In preparation I had written out three pages of narration. I didn't realize I couldn't read them with the lights out. Fortunately I had put the slides in an order that would remind me of what I wanted to say.

I breathed a quick prayer and began to tell my stories about my friends and how they lived and died. I realize now that because I was not rigid in my planned presentation, the Spirit was able to speak through me. I heard myself sharing things I hadn't planned to talk about. I felt "guided," and once I got started the fear left.

Afterward, one woman said, "You know, I've wanted to get involved but I felt I had nothing to offer. You've given me the courage to try something." A man told me he'd felt touched for the first time in his life. I held his hands and he wept. Two people invited me to speak to their organizations: one, a church; the other, a Rotary Club. How had *I* moved people to the point of tears and courage? OK, Lord, I hear you. Thank you.

As weeks went by, it seemed that that was what God wanted me to do. For over two years God had evidently wanted me to comfort the afflicted, and now he was calling me to afflict the comfortable. As I became more relaxed in front of audiences I was freer to express some of my frustrations and concerns, my views of how things got this way and what could be done about it. Many groups and organizations in suburbia wanted to hear what was going on in the ghettos. Some affluent people, wanting someone to be the target for their anger and fear, did not welcome what I had to say. I would notice someone sitting in an audience with arms crossed and a scowl on his or her face as though he were planning a counterattack. If there was a question and answer period at the end of my talk, I knew what to expect. Someone would stand up and say, "If those lazy, no-good _____ would get off their _____ and get a job, they'd have a better life." Or, "Those prostitutes just keep having kids so they can collect Aid for Dependent Children." "Why don't they go back where they belong? Who needs 'em?"

I didn't know how to stand up against that sort of thing. Sometimes I'd get a lump in my throat and feel tears welling up in my eyes. I wanted to cry because I loved the people I was working with and I wanted to love the ones I was speaking to. I had visions of being in front of a firing squad at times, when a hostile person lashed out at me as though I represented the black population. It hurt.

I began to realize that I needed to learn some things about communication. I had thought it was hard to relate to those in the ghetto—well, let me tell you, it seemed even harder to communicate with the upper middle class. I couldn't get them to *feel*.

During a long night when I couldn't sleep, I picked up my guitar and composed a song that expressed some of my frustration.

How can I make them hear, Lord?
How can I make them see?
How can I make the wealthy know there's poverty?
I don't just mean the money,
I mean the poor tired souls.
I wonder how it feels, Lord, to not reach any goals.

How can I show them hunger?
How can I make them care?
When they've got so much and still don't want to share!
How can I tell 'em what love is?
I don't even think they feel!
My God, how will they know you if they never stop
to kneel?

I know just how you felt, Lord,
When they hung you on that tree.
'cause when I try to warn them, I fear they'll do it to me.
My Lord, I'm gettin' tired.
My God, I'm gettin' weak.
But I know that I'll see heaven if just your face I seek.
Thank you, Lord.

I really have no choice, Lord,
But to follow you.

But O my God, I need you to show me what to do!
How can I wake up people?
Do I have to start a riot?
They don't even know what's happenin' when they're
sittin' home so quiet!

How can I make them hear, Lord?
How can I make them see?
How can I make the wealthy know there's poverty?
Have mercy on the wealthy!
They've got their problems too!
O my God, forgive them . . . for they know not what
they do.
Mercy, Lord.

Each time I prayed about whether I was to accept another speaking engagement the answer seemed to be yes, even though my speaking to so many groups meant that I no longer had time to visit my friends in the inner city as often.

I didn't know statistics or percentages or budgets or government programs and the like. All I knew was what I had experienced, what I had felt. I could try to relate how I thought the people living in the ghetto felt and something about how they lived, but I never tried to become an authority on racism or poverty. So I continued to speak to groups of all kinds: civic clubs, teachers, Sunday school teachers, librarians, Girl Scouts, church congregations, probation officers, ministers, on and on.

I was determined to find ways to communicate to the upper middle class and become more creative in my presentations. I tried to dramatize some of the situations I had found in the city so that people might share the feelings. That seemed essential to me if they were to understand. I remember telling an audience about a dead man I found in an old hotel. One of my students had lived in room 301 and I had gone to visit her several times before one day when she had failed to show up for class. I knocked on the door several times and got no answer. Just as I was about to leave, I thought I could hear a radio playing inside. Thinking she might have fallen asleep, I turned the doorknob and opened the door. An old man lay sprawled on the couch. I strained to focus my eyes to see a sign of what I sensed. He looked lifeless. I quickly closed the door and shivered. What should I do? I wanted to run. Did I dare just leave him there without telling anybody?

With shaky knees and trembling voice I knocked on the door of room 303 and said, "Pardon me, but there is a man in the next room and I think he's dead." They said they didn't know him and closed the door. Hey, you can't do that, I thought. What am I supposed to do with him? I decided to try once more and I knocked on the door across from his. For some reason I said, "Your neighbor in 301 needs help." The response was, "Tell the manager." I returned to the man's door and felt the need to peek in one more time. Please, God, resurrect him, because I don't know what to do!

He just lay there.

I rang the bell next to the manager's door and was asked what I wanted by a sort of shabby man. Although I tried to explain the problem to him, he gave the impression that since the man's rent was paid up, he didn't care what was happening in his room.

What do you do with a dead man whom nobody cares about? I wondered if he had any family, if he'd even be missed. I felt a need to get out of the dingy building, so I began to walk and walk as I prayed for guidance. Six blocks from the hotel, I found an old church (the church we'd been working in had no one there that day). I wandered in, almost afraid I'd find someone. I wasn't eager to repeat the story since I had felt so foolish the other times. A priest was in the office, so I told him. He assured me he would call the authorities. I was relieved that someone had at least heard me. I prayed that God would look over the situation and I asked his forgiveness for my not even thinking to pray for the old man.

I also grieved over the loss of my student, a friend I'd come to love. She must have moved out in the night, as so many did when their rent was overdue.

I also told my audiences about an old black woman who was hemorrhaging so much she couldn't walk. I asked her who her doctor was. She had no doctor. I asked to use her phone. She had no phone. Who in her family could I get in touch with? She had no family. There was no way I could walk away from her apartment and leave her there, but what could I do? What would Dan say if I ever brought someone like her home! I wrapped old dirty towels around her and put her in my car, determined to get help, and ended up at the county hospital.

It was overwhelming. I couldn't find the entrance. It seemed like hours before I got her inside the doors, where we were told to wait. We waited, waited, waited. People who came in after us were eventually taken care of before we were even questioned. We couldn't fill out the forms, because she didn't know any of the answers. I felt retarded. Sick people lined the hall—some on the floor, some in wheelchairs, some groaning, some drunk. It was a nightmare. Why wasn't I more assertive?

I felt anger welling up inside. Why won't someone help us? This shouldn't even be my problem. Take her, somebody. Why don't I speak up? Why am I so cowardly? I found myself hoping she'd scream so someone would take her away and I'd be free to go. How could I leave her there? How will she ever get home? How did I get into this?

I saw blood soaking through the towels held in place by her wrinkled black hands and I was afraid she'd die if something wasn't done soon. I looked at my watch and realized I had stayed so long I wouldn't be able to get home by dinnertime. Oh, no! I have to get out of here!

I finally got enough gumption to go up to a window and tell the nurse my situation. She repeated what I had heard her say 200 times before, that they were very busy but would get to her when they could. I said goodbye to the old woman and left. Dear God, will they ever get to her? Who will pay for her treatment? Who will take her home? Or go to her funeral? How do I get myself into these things? Again I left the inner city feeling hollow, hurting, angry.

In my talks I found myself going into details like those about a person, a relationship, rather than generalizing or giving facts or conclusions. My goals were to awaken people to the needs of people less fortunate, to awaken people to the possibilities within themselves to participate in the healing of the world. I hoped to inspire them to muster up courage to try something new, to risk something for the sake of helping someone. Here I was doing so many things I never thought I could do, discovering that love and encouragement and hope are what the underprivileged need most. It didn't matter to me if members of my audiences volunteered for duty in the inner city or a rest home or their church or wherever. My dream was that they would begin to care enough, feel competent enough, to reach out to someone, whether a neighbor, elderly person, depressed person, or child.

Not everyone needs to go far away from home to learn to love. It just so happens, I did.

PART TWO
My Throat Problem

CHAPTER 9

Many people in my audiences were curious about how my
involvement was affecting my family and my home. Occasionally a woman would come up to me after a presentation and say, "I could *never* do something like that; my
husband would never let me," or, "You must have a
wonderful husband if he lets you run around like that."

Well, it was true I had a wonderful husband, but let me
assure you that there is a price to pay for everything. He
and I were slipping way behind in our own relationship.
Many feelings were being put on the shelf to wait for
times that never came. Once, during a heated argument
over my being gone so much, Dan said, "You've changed!
You're not the girl I married!"

I knew he was right. I wasn't the same. Should I feel
guilty? Should I try to change back? Is that even possible?
What would God think of that? How did God expect me to
follow him and still keep a marriage together?

I'm sure Dan felt that he had lost me to another love. I
could understand his feelings but I didn't know what to
do about it. "God, I've trusted you with my life. Help me
to trust you with the consequences."

My speaking continued for the next two years, averaging
four talks a week. Some of them were morning meetings,
some luncheons. About twice a week I was gone in the

evening. I tried to keep up with our social life so that I would be spending some time with Dan, which meant that we bowled in the church bowling league, played bridge, attended a couples' group at the church, and took in an occasional movie. Obviously I wasn't home very often.

I gradually phased out of my inner-city and Willowbrook involvement, which seemed to please my family. I was home a little more. Others from Garden Grove continued to visit and assist for a while after I stopped going.

By 1969, I had spoken to over 500 groups and I had some real tests during that time. Tension seemed to be mounting in our marriage. I recall one time in particular. I was booked up for three months, and Dan was going through a difficult time on the job. He hadn't been feeling well physically, and he was lonely and depressed. He may have tried to share his feelings with me but I hadn't "heard" them. Perhaps I had learned how not to hear things I was unable to respond to. We were living almost totally separate lives.

After a gall bladder operation, Dan spent weeks at home recuperating. I was gone every day. He felt stuck with the kids and probably unloved. Shortly after returning to work he had an incisional hernia. Back to the hospital for corrective surgery. Another recuperating period of six weeks.

I was caught on a fast moving merry-go-round and I couldn't get off. These speaking engagements had been scheduled six months ago. How did I know that Dan would need me? How could I cancel them without notice? Besides, I felt that God had led me to say Yes to each place. I was in the habit of saying, "Lord, where do you want me to share next?" and each time I would get an invitation.

I felt myself turning to plastic at home so that I wouldn't feel the guilt that was building in me. I stopped telling Dan about the events of my day, since there was no way he could be excited about my activities away from him. I was afraid to ask him about his day because it gave him a chance to tell me how depressed he was and that everything had gone wrong. I felt guilty if the boys had caused any problems—like spilling something or needing transportation or wrestling or wanting lunch. I became a robot. Even on days when I had no plans, I found myself thinking of excuses to be gone so that I wouldn't have to face him. All the while I was pretending that nothing was wrong, that I was happy. Finally Dan returned to work. He was probably relieved to be out of the house, but undoubtedly he was insecure about "us."

Still, I couldn't believe it when another check-up revealed that he'd had another incisional hernia and would be in the hospital again. That year he was home a total of 100 days and I resented every one of them. I vacillated between guilt and resentment. One day I'd feel guilty that I wasn't dropping everything and caring for him "like a good wife should." The next day I would shift to resenting his being so incapacitated that I felt needed by him.

I again joined a prayer group so I'd have an excuse to be gone on Monday mornings. Every week the women would pray for him, which helped relieve some of my guilt for not praying for him more. I would listen to their lovely prayers and think to myself, "It's easy for you to love him; you don't have to live with him."

One day when I returned from my prayer group at noon, I found Dan lying on the sofa. He looked gray. He gasped, "My heart, my heart . . . feel it. Something's wrong." He felt faint, he said, and couldn't stand up. What could I do? Dan weighs over 200 pounds! Yes, call the doctor, that's what I should do! Dr. Jones? This is Mrs. Zakich. Something's wrong with Dan. His heart is pounding so fast and he's weak and can hardly talk. What should I do? Bring him in? OK, we'll be right in. Goodbye. Hey, wait a minute! I can't lift him! Help!

It's amazing what you can do when you're scared! Somehow I got him to his feet and supported him until he collapsed in the car and we arrived at the doctor's office, where they took him immediately. After a brief look, Dr. Jones said, "Call the Rescue Squad," to one of the nurses. What are they doing to him? I wondered as four people in white worked on him. Someone said, "Get him to the hospital," and the next hour became a nightmare. I couldn't think. I couldn't hope. I don't remember how I got to the hospital. In the emergency room I was jerked out of

my daze when I heard someone say the word *coronary*. O
God, he's had a heart attack. I had never said those words
before. It can't be. Not Dan! He's so young! I don't know
how to handle this! God? O God, don't let him die!

I wanted to remind God that we were not at a very good
point in our relationship but I felt too ashamed to mention
that. Did I cause the attack? I'm sorry if I did. Lord, I'm all
mixed up. Where did I go wrong?

"All right, Mrs. Zakich, you can go in," a voice said. I
shook my head to face reality as I walked behind a nurse
down a long corridor to a room filled with equipment.
There in an oxygen tent was Dan. In my insides I was
screaming, "I'm sorry, I'm sorry," but on the outside I
slowly reached out and patted his foot and mouthed,
"You'll be OK." I felt awkward looking at him as if he was
an animal in a cage. I didn't know what to do. How tragic
it seemed, that I didn't know what to do!

Suddenly a thought came to me. The kids! Where are
the kids? I had locked the door and left in such haste that
I hadn't arranged for them. What would they do when
they came home from school and found no one there?
That had never happened before. Oh good heavens, I've
got to run. Goodbye, dear. I must go find the boys. I'll be
back at visiting hours. O God, this doesn't seem right, but I
don't know what to do.

I drove home feeling like a lousy wife and a horrible
mother. I fought to keep out the thought, "What if he
dies?" I found Dean and Darin at a neighbor's and tried to
explain what had happened without worrying them too
much. I wished I could believe what I told them. They
seemed satisfied that God would take care of Daddy and
spent the evening doing the things they usually did. I was
permitted to talk to Dan on the phone, and even though he
said his heart had settled down, my fear wouldn't allow
me to trust that the worst was over. They would be putting
him through a battery of tests in the morning.

It seemed strange to go to bed without Dan beside me.
The only other time we had been apart at night was when
I was at the retreat. I had a strange remorse that I had
chosen to leave him for the retreat, but I quickly blocked
the feeling. There were too many undealt-with emotions

inside me to risk allowing even one to come out, for fear they'd *all* come out.

I called the hospital in the middle of the night and was told that Dan was resting quietly and that visiting hours were at one P.M. tomorrow. Something hit me like a bolt of lightning! Tomorrow. San Bernardino. I almost forgot. I was scheduled to speak at a breakfast at six A.M., which meant I'd have to get up at four in order to get dressed and drive the seventy miles to get there in time. The woman in charge had just called me that morning to tell me that 300 people were expected, including the mayor, council members, and various civic leaders. They had done elaborate publicity with newspaper articles and posters. They had printed fancy programs and so on. Oh, no! I had planned on Dan's being home in the morning to get the boys up and off to school. What am I going to do!

I knew I needed to pray, but for some reason I couldn't. I felt abandoned by God. Hurt. Everything seemed confusing, overwhelming, outside of God's plan.

A look at the clock made me realize that I would have to figure this one out myself, since two o'clock in the morning is not a popular time to discuss business or problems. I decided to pray. "Heavenly Father, where are you? Did you go away? Did *I* go away? I'm scared and mixed up. What should I do? Lord, do you want me to stay home tomorrow or should I go and fulfill the promise I made to speak? Would it seem that I don't love Dan if I go, Lord? You *know* I love him. Help *him* to know it, Lord. I know *you* love him, too, more that I ever could. O God, I *must* know by morning what to do." At some point I fell asleep with a prayer on my lips, and I slept soundly until I was awakened by a violent rainstorm. It was three-thirty A.M.

I wandered through the house, hoping to hear God's voice clearly telling me what to do. The thought occurred to me that I'd been willing to trust God with my life (as best I knew how to let go of it) so why couldn't I trust God with Dan's life? Wouldn't it seem like a lack of faith if I stayed home and called the hospital every hour to check on him? Of course! If I really trusted God, I could leave him in charge of Dan. To show how much I trusted him, I decided in that moment to go ahead and go to San Bernardino. Visiting hours were not until one o'clock in the afternoon, and I expected to be back by nine A.M. OK, Lord, I'll go. I trust you with Dan. I trust your healing power.

I decided to get the boys up and take them with me. They would miss only an hour of school if I got them back by nine. Dean thought the world must be coming to an end when I shook him and tried to explain what was going to take place. Darin groaned and said he wanted to sleep. Dean said he was sick. I felt his head and discovered that he had a fever. Why does everything seem so much more complicated in real life than when I plan it in my mind? If I'm going to trust God with my husband, can I trust him with my son who has a 103° temperature? As I rolled the boys up in blankets, I kept reminding God, I'm trusting you! I'm trying to be obedient. I'm not doing this because I want to! I'm doing this for you, Lord. Nobody else.

The blinding rain made it almost impossible for me to see the white line on the road. The boys slept in the back seat and I worked hard to keep negative thoughts and fears from entering my mind. I couldn't help but question, though, why, if God wanted me to be obedient, were there so many obstacles? I continued to drive despite the strong desire to go back home, jump in my cozy bed, cover up my head, and sleep until all this was over. We arrived three minutes before someone introduced me, which was just enough time to find a lounge where the boys could sit and wait for me. "Our speaker today is a courageous woman [if they only knew] who is a living demonstration of her love [I hope they never ask Dan] and who joyfully serves God by her willingness to give of herself, unselfishly, to all those around her." (I expected one of my boys to stagger through the door with his blanket and cry, "She's mean!") "Mrs. Rhea Zakich . . ."

I took the microphone and tried to act relaxed and cool. I heard myself say, "I'm here because God led me here. This is not an easy time for me and I covet your prayers for my husband and for our whole family." I told them that Dan was in the hospital at that very moment and that I feared it was a heart attack, although the doctors weren't sure yet. Someone suggested that we pray right then, and 300 people laid down their forks and stopped chewing long enough to ask God's healing power to minister to Dan. It was beautiful. I knew when I finished my talk that I had done the right thing. There was a peace and a joy in me as I drove home. I didn't realize it at the time but I was going to have a terrible time explaining what I had done to Dan, to my relatives, and to anyone who had just seen it from the "outside."

As I left San Bernardino, the rain stopped and I wasn't totally surprised when we saw a rainbow. Thank you, Lord. We seemed to hit every green light all the way home and I could hardly wait to get to the phone to call the hospital.

"I'd like to know the condition of Dan Zakich," I said to the operator at the hospital switchboard. "One moment, please," was her response. I felt like an antenna searching for a sound wave as I waited. And then, "He is waiting to go home, ma'am. You may pick him up anytime."

I immediately corrected her by saying, "No, I mean the Dan Zakich in intensive care with the coronary" (O me of little faith).

"One moment, please." Then, "Ma'am, he is ready to be dismissed and is waiting for his wife to pick him up." O God! You're wonderful! I love you! Thank you, God. Thank you, Jesus. Thank you, Holy Spirit. Thank you, people in San Bernardino who prayed for him. Thank you everybody.

I rushed to the room where Dan was sitting on a bed ready to go home. They couldn't explain it but his heart-beat and breathing had become perfectly normal. None of the tests revealed anything abnormal. They were still waiting for the results of a test to see if there was any heart damage, but I had no fears about that. I knew in my heart that a miracle had taken place and that things had happened according to a plan I couldn't understand. But I was learning I could trust it. I felt as if I had passed some sort of test. I had been able to trust God with my family. Little did I know that the tests would get harder and that a very big one was to come shortly.

CHAPTER 10

My speaking continued and things seemed to be going fine except for a sore throat that was starting to irritate me. I'd had a lot of them lately but hadn't gone to the doctor since my calendar was so booked. This time it was terrible, like strep throat or, more accurately, like you feel after a tonsillectomy. It became difficult to swallow and I sounded hoarse.

I asked my prayer group to pray for me and tried to trust that I would be healed. Once I had decided to trust God, I felt as though I couldn't call the doctor or that would indicate a lack of faith. I kept thinking, "It will go away tomorrow," or, "I'll give it one more day." I studied my calendar and picked a date four weeks away, when my obligations let up a little, as the time to call a specialist *if* it hadn't gone away by then.

There were times when it was so sore and the laryngitis so bad that I had to touch a microphone to my lips and whisper to my audiences. Finally I had no choice but to make an appointment with a throat specialist. My voice had become a coarse, raspy squeak and I could still hardly swallow. I was sure that a specialist who was up-to-date on all the cures would simply give me a pill and perhaps suggest that I rest my voice and I'd be well.

As I drove to the doctor I prayed, "Lord, you know I'm

out there doing your work so you'd better fix this up or I'll have to quit." I really didn't have any great concern, just a sense of being inconvenienced.

I watched the doctor's face as he examined my throat. He probed and studied and probed and pressed. I watched his forehead wrinkle and the corners of his mouth drop as he finished his inspection. Very seriously he shook his head, pushed away on his little stool, dropped his hands in his lap, and spoke. "Mrs. Zakich, I don't know if this is going to be hard for you or not since I don't know you and I don't know what you do. But I must tell you to go home and cancel everything on your calendar and announce to your family, and to anyone else who needs to know, that you cannot make a single sound for one month. I want to see you in thirty days and I want nothing to come out of your mouth during that time." He said further that if I accidentally spoke I'd have to start counting from that day. I was to start the next morning.

When those words went into my ears, my first thought was, he has the wrong patient. It can't be me that he's telling that to, because I'm doing God's will and speaking. Then I noticed the frown on his forehead and I realized that he was talking to me. He said that after the inflammation and infection had cleared up, he could do some tests to get a better idea of what the problem was.

I sat and stared. My body seemed numb. How on earth can I be silent for a month when my kids ask me two thousand questions a day, and the phone rings a hundred times a day, and I ask Dan seventy-five questions a day, and . . .

I left the doctor's office to enter a new experience, a very different lifestyle. One of complete silence. One that was to test my faith.

As I drove home, my world began to crumble. The first thing I thought about was the boys, nine and ten at the time. How could they get along without my input? My head began to spin with the things I always needed to say to them. "Brush your teeth, comb your hair, button your shirt, tie your shoes, wear a sweater, shut the door, don't let the dog out, bring in your bike, don't forget your lunch,

quit biting your nails, where's your homework? And
please, stop teasing your brother." How could I be a
mother if I couldn't say those things?

My next thought was, "How can I be a *wife*? What sort
of relationship will we have if I can't talk? Would we even
have one?" Dan had never been very talkative to me.
Would he tell me anything if I couldn't ask him?

Then my mind went to my calendar. Twenty-six speaking engagements strewn out over the next three months.
How could I get out of those? How I dreaded telling the
program committees. Telling? I wouldn't be telling them
anything.

It will seem so impersonal, I thought, for them to receive
a letter after we'd probably spent an hour on the phone or
in person setting the program up. Somehow I managed to
jockey through the heavy afternoon traffic with my mind
somewhere else.

One by one, thoughts came to me as to how this was
going to affect my life. I was almost home when a lump in
my throat blocked out the soreness and tenderness I'd
been experiencing for weeks. I wanted to cry . . . but I
don't cry, I thought. I hadn't cried for years. I prided
myself for being so in control that I never fell apart. What
was this strangling in my throat?

I had been raised at a time and in a family where
feelings were never expressed. Emotions were down-
played, at least the sad or negative ones. I remember as a
child being told so many times, "Don't cry! Don't be a
baby! Be a big girl." If I was hurt, someone would say,
"Oh, that couldn't hurt!" If I felt sad, someone was right
there to tell me it was foolish and that I'd get over it by
tomorrow. If I was lonely or left out, I was told that I
shouldn't feel that way, that I had lots of friends who just
happened to be busy at that time. I was never allowed to
be afraid or embarrassed or angry—not if I was a nice little
girl. So I learned in my childhood that feelings were
dumb. People aren't supposed to have them. And if they
do, they certainly don't let anyone know. Now my eyes
started to blur as the impact of a month of silence began to
hit me. I felt as if a gallon of tears was waiting behind

each eye, pressing against my eyelids, wanting to flow like
Niagara Falls—but I couldn't let that happen. I might have
an accident.

These thoughts occurred on the freeway during rush
hour. I continued driving and swallowing as though I had
seaweed in my throat, blinking as though I was repeatedly
having to push down the cap on a warm bottle of carbon-
ated pop. Thank God, there's the driveway. Now I can go
in and be consoled by my family. As I turned off the
ignition, I saw a scene in my mind of me running into my
husband's arms and crying, having him tell me it'll be all
right, having my children say, "Mommy, we'll be good
and help you."

Oh, the frustration of arriving home to find unexpected
guests visiting. Why did they have to stop by on this
evening? I opened the front door and stood there, trying to
throw all the necessary internal switches to turn me into
the plastic person I'd been most of my life. I certainly
didn't want these casual friends to know I had emotions.
So somehow, I managed to bury the hurt and fear. When I
was asked, "What did the doctor say?" by my husband, I
calmly responded, "Oh, he told me not to talk for a
month."

I wondered why the couple laughed, and then I could
have sworn I saw a grin under Dan's beard. A strange
emptiness swept through me. One of the men went over to
Dan and said, "Congratulations. Where did you find the
doctor? Maybe I can make an appointment for my wife!"
Everyone burst into more laughter. How could they joke at
a time like that? Couldn't they sense that my world was
crumbling? Didn't they care?

I excused myself and raced into the bedroom, dreading
having to return to that circus in the kitchen. Where were
the sympathetic words? Where were the embrace and the
comforting?

My next question was interrupted by the boys racing
into the bedroom and asking what the doctor had said.
Because they showed such interest, and because I'd been
wounded by the others, I got down on my knees and said
in a soft voice, "Children, come here. Mommy has some-

thing to tell you." They stopped dead in their tracks and then walked slowly toward me with a serious look on their faces.

I shook as I took their chins in my hands and said in a shaky voice, "Now you're going to have to be brave. It's bad news." Their eyes were big as saucers as they listened to me say that their mother wouldn't be allowed to talk for one month. Before I could finish telling them how we could get through it if we were all brave, they burst into a cheer, leaped into the air, grabbed each other, and ran from the room. The last words I heard them say were, "Yea! Let's go tell Jimmy and Donnie and Bruce and Stuart!" I was dumbfounded. What is this celebration? Where is the understanding?

I don't remember much else about the evening. I eventually returned to the guests and we ate dinner. I must have helped Darin and Dean get ready for bed as I always did. I might have even read to them. I do recall standing at the kitchen sink scouring a greasy skillet late at night as Dan made a list of things to do in the morning.

1. Call the phone company and have the phone disconnected.

2. Make a "Do Not Disturb" sign for the front door.

3. Call the relatives from work.

4. Buy a large chalkboard and a large box of chalk for Rhea.

5. Go to the library and check out some books to read.

I wanted so desperately to share my feelings with somebody but there didn't seem to be anyone around who was interested. Just when I started to say something to Dan, he announced that he was going to bed since he had to get up early. I stayed up and wrote a few notes before going to bed. Then I lay awake for hours feeling forsaken and forlorn, as though it was my last night on earth and everyone had gone to sleep. Morning eventually came and I was awakened by my sons running into the room to donate their crayons, tablets, and Mickey Mouse Magic Slate. Fortunately, they were old enough to read.

The silence began. The first days I felt challenged. I mentally put on a warrior suit and set out to conquer. I've always been able to make a game out of the distasteful things in life in order to endure them. So that's what I did on my first silent day. I entered into the arena to be the best mute ever.

My enthusiasm lasted for half a day. While the boys were in school and Dan was at work, I wrote many notes and I made lists on a chalkboard. I looked out the window and watched for the mail. I listened to the radio, then watched an afternoon TV show (I had given up my soap operas). When the boys came home from school, they stuck their heads in the door and yelled, "Hi, Mom! We're goin' down to Jimmy's. Bye."

Hey, wait a minute. I have some notes for you, I shouted in my head. You can't play until you've done the chores I wrote on the chalkboard, I yelled mentally as I saw them leaping over the juniper bushes in the yard. No fair. I've waited for you all day.

My sons quickly learned that never to look at the chalkboard was never to have any responsibility. Their posture actually changed. They began to walk around with their heads down so they never had to respond to my charades or the faces I would make as I mouthed my messages.

When Dan arrived home from the office I experienced even more frustration. He always had a routine when he walked through the door and even this day was no exception. The door opens and he says "Hi, Hon. I'm home." I raced into the room. Then he says, "How'd it go today?" to which I shrug my shoulders. I always felt stupid when I realized he wasn't looking at me as he walked to the bedroom where he ritualistically kicked off his shoes.

His next utterance comes as he's rumbling the closet door and looking at his sport shirts. "Where are the kids?" This time I would have to push my way into the pants-section of the closet to go through the gestures of trying to communicate, "Down at Jimmy's." "Was there any mail?" "What's for dinner?"

I realized in the days to come that those questions didn't require answers. They were his way of saying simply, "Hi, I'm home." When I stopped trying to gesture the answers, he didn't even notice.

By the third day, frustration was beginning to set in. I had to face the fact that I couldn't call the boys to come in from playing, couldn't tell them to start their homework, couldn't correct them or give them any instructions. I threw away so many notes no one had read that I felt wasteful as well as neglected. Sometimes I became poetic and artistic on the chalkboard and would put it in a place where they just had to notice it. Still, as I turned out the lights to go to bed, it would remind me of an epitaph on a tombstone with no flowers adorning it.

My sensitivity to noises began to increase. Especially the sounds of the cookie jar lid. Even crumbs dropping on the floor and Kool-Aid dripping off the bottom of a glass seemed to make a noise. Then there were the noisier noises, like the backyard gate when it didn't click the second click, followed by one of the neighbors saying, "Your dog's out." Or a shoe hitting the bedroom wall or a crash in the garage, followed by a "I'm gonna tell Mom."

The next few weeks I thought I was getting a glimpse of what hell must be like. I was in a world, but I couldn't participate. It was as if I were invisible. I couldn't affect anything. Everything began to irritate me. Noises, conversations, laughter, TV, being alone, watching the neighbors enjoying themselves chatting on the lawn, not being able to holler down the hall or respond when I heard the boys plotting some scheme.

One night, about the third week, it got the best of me. I couldn't sleep. The boys had bounced the basketball in the living room and broken my favorite figurine, a statue of a young girl kneeling with her face turned up to God and her hands cupped in her lap. On the underside the caption said, "Here I am, Lord; send me." It was the crushing blow; the straw that made the load too heavy. Maybe it was the way my son reported it: "Hey, Mom. This guy's head fell off." I fell apart inside. This is too hard, Lord! Why are you doing this to me? Did I do something wrong? Lord, are you there?

I paced the floor until well after midnight. Frustration turned to anger. Red-hot anger. Every time I thought of God, the anger increased. Where was he in this? I just couldn't match it all up with the God who had seemed so loving. The God who had been guiding me. I became enraged. See if I ever do another thing for you! I shouted in my mind. I went on to remind him of all the things I had done on his behalf in the last few years. Lord, I went to the inner city for you and then was willing to go out and speak to all those scary groups because I thought you wanted me to. This doesn't make sense! Now you take my voice from me! Why? Why? No response.

To scream so loud inside your head and not get any sign that it's been heard by anyone seemed devasting. I collapsed in a chair, exhausted and confused. I began to get in touch with the feeling that was down under the anger: the hurt at that huge rejection from God. Where do you go when God rejects you? I wondered. I decided that I'd have to put all thoughts of God out of my mind if I was to be able to go on. Maybe he doesn't even exist. Maybe it's all just in people's heads. Whatever—it didn't matter now. I was never going to church again and I was never going to pray anymore.

I closed the door on God that night and went to bed without saying goodbye to the Companion I'd had through so many experiences.

CHAPTER 11

The remainder of the month was painful mentally and emotionally. I stopped writing notes. I stopped smiling and doing my charades to communicate. I stopped looking for the mail everyday. Nothing seemed to matter.

The furor inside continued to rage. When I saw people laughing. When someone said something I didn't understand and I couldn't say, "Huh?" When I saw Dan seeming to enjoy himself reading. It made me furious that none of my friends had the gumption to rip the Do Not Disturb sign off the door and say "Forget it! I want to see you!"

I learned some interesting things about anger during my silence. One discovery was that anger is no "fun" at all if nobody knows you're mad. The few people I saw all seemed to think I wanted to be cheered up. They'd tell me jokes and clown around while I forced myself to respond. Inside, I didn't want to laugh. I wanted to cry.

I wished that someone, anyone, would give me a sign that he knew how difficult this was for me, that I felt lonely and left out of life. No one did. I felt as if I could have lain on the floor in a fetal position and people would have ignored me.

I saw very few friends that month. The word must have spread that I couldn't talk, and perhaps the sign on the door and the disconnected phone communicated that I didn't want company.

I also felt horrendous guilt because I had stopped going to the inner city. In many people's minds, I would now be in the category of those who come to them, make great promises, and then disappear. There was no way I could have gotten to them since they didn't have phones and the doctor had said, "Start tomorrow." So I felt trapped, and it wasn't my fault.

I spent time each day writing letters to the organizations that had invited me to speak, trying to explain why I couldn't come and trying to cover up my guilt feelings with extra words. I couldn't help but remember the one phone call I had made the night I announced to my family that I wouldn't be talking for a month. I was to speak the very next day to a church women's group in a nearby city, so I had to cancel that engagement by phone. It was awful. "Mrs._____, this is Rhea Zakich, and I won't be able to speak tomorrow . . ." Before I could finish, she said, "What? Well, what am I supposed to do? You promised to be there and there will be 100 women there with programs with your picture on them. This really leaves me in a predicament. It's too late to get someone else. I wish you would have given me more notice!" I fell apart inside. I felt guilty that I was having throat trouble. I was hurt because I thought I was the one who should get the sympathy, and instead here I was feeling the need to console her. I felt like a wounded soldier who had crawled up to someone to ask for help and got hit on the head with a rifle butt.

Only three more days. Two. One. I went to the doctor on the thirtieth day feeling proud inside that I hadn't said a single word. I walked into the treatment room expecting to be congratulated and praised. The doctor would marvel at the progress.

He sat down on his little rolling stool, took a tongue depressor and some sort of long scope, and began to investigate. I watched every face muscle and tried to interpret his changes of expression. I strained to see a reflection in his glasses of what he was seeing, but to no avail. Finally, after what seemed like an eternity, he spoke. "I'm afraid we're going to have to operate. I'll have Janice call the hospital and make all the arrangements. We'll try to get you in in the morning and, of course, no talking beforehand." Everything inside of me went limp. There was a feeling of disbelief as I looked at him, the same feeling I'd had the month before.

I went home. I was numb. I packed my suitcase, and the next thing I knew I was in the hospital awaiting throat surgery. I didn't know what was wrong with me, and I couldn't even ask. My doctor, a wonderful man, did explain in his medical language what he was going to do, but instead of easing my mind, it caused ninety-six questions to form in my head. Questions that would never be asked, let alone answered.

I was put in a room with three other women who talked incessantly, each describing in gory detail her problem and the operation she was awaiting. One was going to have a tumor removed from her throat and I wondered why she could talk and I wasn't allowed to. After asking me a series of probing questions that I couldn't answer, they decided I was retarded and thereafter left me alone.

The evening seemed long. I tried not to think. I tried not to feel. The TV was blaring and cigarette smoke was hovering over my bed. I stared out in the hall, just for something to do. I tried to guess when someone would walk by. Suddenly there appeared in the doorway a tall handsome priest, all in black. As I was wondering who he was, he asked which one of us was Rhea Zakich. My heart skipped a beat. Who was he and how did he know me?

One of the women pointed to my bed. He walked over and ever so gently explained that he was the husband of one of my Episcopalian friends from my old prayer group. He had come to pray for me. Pray for me? I felt a rush of blood go to my head as I looked at the three women who had stopped talking and were now staring at us. Why did I feel embarrassed? I wasn't familiar with Episcopalians. What did they do when they prayed?

My mind wanted to shout, "I don't believe in God anymore," but my body just lay there. He asked, "Would you like me to pray for you?" I didn't know what that meant. Would he get down on his knees? Would he shout

out loud? The woman next to me sat up on the edge of her
bed expecting the show to begin.

I couldn't seem to shake my head Yes or No, so I
shrugged my shoulders as though to say, "I don't care."
What a shabby response, I thought, the moment I did it. A
wave of humiliation swept through me and I felt immobilized and dumb.

He slowly reached out and put his hand on my throat.
With his beautiful face toward heaven and his other hand
raised as though to receive God's blessings, he began to
pray aloud. For a fleeting moment I thought he must be St.
Francis . . . he seemed so holy. Then my ornery mind
flashed to the other women in the room and I noticed
them watching and listening. Why was I so embarrassed?
"Lord, bless this special child of yours . . ."

I thought, "That proves it. He's got the wrong patient."

"Honor her faith, precious Lord, and heal her body . . ."
His voice faded out when I began my own prayer: "God,
help him to hurry up, get done, and get out of here." I was
sweating as I peeked at the others, who had now turned
down the TV. He finally finished his prayer, squeezed my
hand, and said goodbye. With a sense of relief I covered
my head and fell asleep, my only escape.

Morning came quickly and I was whisked off to surgery
to have some tumor-like growths removed from my vocal
cords. The shock of the operation was nothing compared
to the surprise upon returning to my room to find the
woman who'd had the throat tumor, sitting up in bed,
smiling broadly. When she saw me, she blurted out,
"Praise the Lord! I've been healed! Be sure to tell your
priest friend when you see him that I prayed with him last
night and asked God to heal me. When I was on the
operating table this morning, the doctor said there was no
tumor there. Isn't that wonderful? It was on the X-rays, but
now it's healed. Thank you, Lord."

I felt bitter because I had gone through my surgery,
which meant that the prayer hadn't changed anything for
me. I felt cheated. As the day went on, I thought about
nothing else. I could see why it hadn't happened to me. I
remembered that woman's interest, her eagerness to hear,

her openness, her obvious faith. Somehow I had sabotaged myself. I was heartsick.

Even more frustrated than when I arrived, I left the hospital to go home to thirty more days of silence. I was tired of being angry and having no one notice. Tired of every day seeming the same. Tired of being tired. I became aware during this time that anger takes a tremendous amount of energy. Because I couldn't express the anger, it seemed to be eating me up inside. I felt empty. How can I go another month when I'm shriveling up and dying? I had hoped so much that I could contact all my old friends and my relatives after the first month and find out all the news. I had rehearsed things hundreds of times that I wanted to tell my family. The despair seemed incredible.

I entered my house to begin my new "sentence" with no ambition, no goals, no incentive, no interest. Just time, lots of time. I didn't want to read or watch TV. I didn't want to be around Dan or the kids.

I retreated to our den which is located down a long hall, far removed from our kitchen and living room, the center of all activity. I became a hermit. I didn't want to think, feel, hear, or care about anything.

Self-pity became my enemy as it became more and more evident that the world, and certainly my husband and children, could get along quite well without me. In fact, it seemed as if my boys were happier than they'd ever been. Their quarrels were not as frequent. They were taking more responsibility than they ever had before. It was even evident that learning was taking place without my help or input. Oh, how my ego was suffering. The suspicion that nobody needed me kept me depressed.

I was immobilized in my silence. It was as if I was waiting and waiting for something and couldn't concentrate on anything else. I'd always imagined that if I had any spare time I would read, clean closets, sew, become a gourmet cook. Here I was just sitting and staring. I wondered why it was that, when I could talk, I felt so enthusiastic and energized, and now that I couldn't, I was constantly tired and unmotivated.

CHAPTER 12

Now that I've lived through that time in my life, I'm aware that some very funny things happened—though they didn't seem funny then. On the second or third day of my silence, I was sitting in a rocking chair looking out the window. Darin and Dean ran in from play shouting, "Mommy, Mommy, can we bring Jimmy and Billy and Donny and Stuart in? They want to look at you!" I thought, "Look at me!" But what could I say?

The screen door opened and in strolled a gang of little boys. They stood across the room and stared at me. What were they looking at? What did they expect to see? I realize now that it was probably the first time those kids ever saw me with my mouth shut.

And then something happened that was to be repeated many times in the weeks to come, with adults as well as children. They assumed that, because I couldn't talk, I couldn't hear. While I sat there, eight feet from them, one of them leaned over to another and said, "Does she still eat?" Another one said, "She looks funny, doesn't she?" When Jimmy asked my son if I still went to the bathroom, I'd had enough. I got up and left the room. As I walked toward the hall I heard one whisper, "Maybe she's going now!" When the screen door slammed five times, I knew they'd gone back out to play.

We had a dog that loved to escape every time the front door opened a crack. One morning as the boys left for school, the dog made its getaway. I walked around the neighborhood for an hour and couldn't find her, and of course I couldn't ask for help. Later in the morning as I looked out the front window (my favorite pastime) I saw the dog running down the street with three other dogs of varying sizes. I ran to the door, opened it, and realized that I couldn't call. I whistled my loudest high-school football game whistle. It worked. My dog came running, but so did the other three. In the door bounded what seemed like a wolf pack. How do you communicate with a batch of dogs when you can't make any sounds and they won't look at you? I did everything I could: stomped my feet, made ugly faces, clapped my hands, waved a towel at them. The German shepherd thought I was playing. He jumped into the air, grabbed onto the towel, and pulled me around the room until he won. It took the whole pack of wieners I'd planned for dinner to lure three out and one back in.

Another incident was on a night when I hadn't prepared any dinner. Dan was so beautiful about being willing to take us out to eat if my day had been stressful.

That night we went out for dinner to a coffee shop a few miles from home. The boys chose a booth in the back and sat side by side while Dan and I took our places across from them. I took my tablet and pencil so I could participate somewhat in the conversations. As we waited for our food to come, I noticed my younger son's arm as he rested his chin on his hand. Streaks of dirt looked like they'd been there for quite some time. Would we ever get back to normal so I could remind them to take showers more often? I took my pencil and wrote: "Look at your arms. They're filthy. You MUST take a shower tonight." I handed it to him. He rolled his eyes in disgust and put the note down as our dinners were delivered to us. We had a lovely meal with very little strife.

As we were standing at the cashier's counter waiting to pay the bill, I glanced toward the back of the restaurant just in time to see our waitress pick up the note. She looked frantically at her arms, then shook her head in disbelief. Oh, no! She thinks I left the note for her. I turned and ran to the car, jumped in, and ducked down onto the floor of the back seat. My husband, thinking I had gotten sick, rushed out and sped home for my sake.

Tablet and pencil did not seem to be an effective or adequate form of communication for me. At times writing added to my frustration rather than eased it—partly because nobody waited around long enough for me to respond on paper to their questions. Everyone seemed to move so fast, to be in such a hurry. Public occasions were usually humiliating for me. Sometimes I would see a friend in the crowd and feel excited as she approached. "How are you doing?" she would say. "See you around." There I was, writing "Rotten" on my little tablet, then looking up to see that she'd gone.

Another common happening was the person who would come up, bubbling with enthusiasm, and say, "Hi, Rhea! What have you been doing lately? I bet you watch TV a lot! Or do you read? You always wanted to read. Did you see Hallmark Hall of Fame on TV the other night? I love that actor. Do you like him? Don't you think he's cute? . . ." OK, there were five questions; sometimes there'd be eight or nine. I would always wait until the person finished talking before I'd start to write, so as not to appear rude. So after his or her dissertation, I'd take my little pencil and write, "Not very well. No. Yes. No. Sort of." Looking up I'd see the person talking and laughing with someone else. Depending on how "bruised" I felt that day, I would decide whether or not to go to the friend, tap her on the shoulder, and show her my scrawled paper. Many times when I risked that, she'd look at it with a quizzical look on her face and have to admit that she had forgotten what she'd asked me.

Obviously, to write the entire question for each answer seemed too time-consuming. Very few people were willing or thoughtful enough to ask a simple question and wait until I wrote the answer before going on. Many people seemed to use the questions simply to open the door for them to tell me what was on their own minds. They would expound on their opinion and then say, "Well, it's good seeing you."

I probably shouldn't complain. At least those people knew I could hear. What a strange feeling to be in a crowd and hear yourself being talked about. I'd stare at my hands or my feet. I'd pretend to be reading something or filing my nails. I never knew if I should walk away and give them privacy, or listen and risk embarrassing them if it occurred to them that I could still hear.

Since I dreaded these public appearances by myself, I would cling to my husband's arm: he could explain that I couldn't talk. "How is she?" they would ask Dan, and he, knowing I was under the best medical care, would reply, "Oh, she's fine." Actually, I didn't feel fine at all! I was lonely, hurting, scared, cut off from life. The people might go on to ask if there was anything they could do, or did I need anything, and because Dan really did take good care of me the answer was "Naw, she doesn't need anything. If she does, she writes it down and I get it for her." That was true, but somehow I felt cheated that they hadn't looked at me so I could shake my head or nod or smile or frown.

Once in awhile I'd look down at myself to check out the possibility of my being invisible. And one time I wished I could become invisible. I made the mistake of taking a note into the bank and handing it to a teller, who quickly pushed the silent alarm. Two men suddenly rushed up on either side of me. Security guards.

The realization that nobody really *knew* me began to penetrate. Some of my friends knew what I *thought* about a given thing, what my *opinion* was. But I had never shared my *feelings* with anyone. In a sense, therefore, I was completely alone. The real person I was, was living inside the robot that people had gotten acquainted with. The individual they knew, wasn't really me, but rather was the accumulation of masks and messages I'd learned to show and give to be accepted. How can I get out? How can I let someone in? It's lonely in here! Even my husband didn't know me, and it wasn't his fault. We'd spent almost all of our time together discussing the kids, his job, my social activities. We planned trips, balanced budgets, but didn't talk about our feelings.

Once when I was staring off into space in my rocking chair, my son came up to me, gently touched my face, and said in a soft voice, "Mommy, are you in there?"

The sixtieth day finally arrived, the first day in months that I was eager to get out of bed in the morning. I had watched the calendar and counted the days religiously, and I could hardly wait to get to the doctor's office for my checkup. I had seen this moment many times in my mind: I arrive and am greeted by a cheering crowd. Someone presents me with a gold trophy for being the first woman to accomplish such a feat under such trying circumstances . . .

I was led to a treatment room where I sat and waited, feeling smug. I did it! I did it! He'll see.

The doctor finally came in and did his usual probing and studying. I watched his forehead hoping to read the wrinkles, but they didn't match up with the slight smile on his lips. As my mind was saying, "Well, am I OK or not?" he spoke. "Your throat seems to be healing nicely. It looks like you've been very obedient about being quiet. I'll have my office call the hospital and arrange for surgery in the morning, so we can take care of the other side . . . "
I couldn't believe it. I felt tricked. How could this be happening when I didn't know there were two sides to whatever he was doing in there! My heart sank. I can't do it, I thought. I can't live through any more of this. But none of those feelings found expression.

The next thing I knew I was entering the hospital with my little suitcase like an obedient child. Although I was in a room by myself this time, I still couldn't sleep. Fears began to creep in. I bet I have cancer. I bet I'm dying and nobody is telling me. Maybe that was why many old friends had stopped coming around . . . because they knew. I became paranoid. The nurses talking in the hall made me suspicious that secrets were being kept from me.

To whom could I turn? Who even knew that I felt troubled and scared? How alone I felt. I couldn't turn to God since I had written him off last month.

The operation took place, and two more growths were removed. I lived through it—much to my surprise. Actually the operation was the easy part. Living with the consequences was much harder. When the time came for my dismissal, there were some mix-ups: missing signatures, misplaced records, etc. Dan had come to pick me up, but since things were delayed he decided to wait in the car.

It was a beautiful sunny morning. The doctor insisted on accompanying me to the car, which was parked at the far end of the hospital parking lot. He put his arm around me and told me in a calm, soothing voice that everything seemed to go well and that I was a good patient. What *choice* did I have? I thought. I wondered what it would be like to kick and scream and pound and cuss, which is what part of me really wanted to do.

I suddenly became aware that he'd stopped. "Mrs. Zakich, I have something I want to say to you and I'm not quite sure how to say it," he said. My heart began to race. I felt my temperature rise as I looked at him with my most questioning expression. "I don't want to frighten you but I do feel I should level with you," he went on. Oh, no! Here it comes. Bad news. Where's Dan? "I hope you're not just sitting around the house waiting for this to be over" (which is exactly what I'd been doing), "since we won't really know much until after thirty more days of silence, Mrs. Zakich . . ."

My head felt like an echo chamber as I tried to focus my eyes. He looked down at his hands and then back to me. "I can't guarantee at this point that you'll ever get your voice back." My head began to spin. I leaned against a parked car and felt life slowly drain from my body. "I don't think there's anything to worry about, but I would suggest that you give some thought as to what you might do if you are a mute." A mute? I can't be a mute! You can't do this to me!

The doctor led me to the car and opened the door. There was Dan, patiently waiting while listening to the radio. He hadn't heard and I couldn't tell him. As he greeted me warmly and filled me in on everything the kids had done while I'd been gone, my mind was yelling, "Thirty more days! Thirty more days! I might never talk again!" I felt suspended in some strange time capsule. I couldn't hear, see, or think. My mind pushed a button that said "fast-forward" and I was frantically trying to see into the future.

I don't remember the drive home. I didn't have a tablet or pencil so there was no way I could communicate what the doctor had said. Dan continued his report. Darin had cleaned the kitchen, I had gotten some mail, he'd gone to the store, the neighbors took out the shrubs in their front yard . . .

We arrived at the house and Dan was uncertain whether to go to work (it was ten-thirty in the morning) or to stay home with me. As we went in the front door he asked, "Do you need me to stay home or should I go to the office?" How do I answer that, I thought? "Well, what do you think? Do you feel OK?" How can I tell him what I think or how I feel? I stood motionless trying to process the data and my capabilities. I really *was* OK. I guess I don't really *need* him, I thought. I decided to nod Yes to whatever he asked next, and it was, "Well, then, should I go to work?" He gave me a kiss, said he'd be home at dinnertime as usual, and left.

CHAPTER 13

The moment I closed the door, I was gripped by a wave of panic unlike anything I'd ever felt. Every cell in my body seemed electrified. The impact of what the doctor said hit me full blast. What my mind retained was, "You might never talk again." What it didn't remember was, "Now this isn't for certain. I just want you to be thinking about the possibility."

I remember running all through the house in a frenzy. It seems crazy, but I was then beyond thinking rationally. I recall racing up and down the hall, looking in every room, opening doors, cupboards, drawers. In my mind I was shouting, "What am I going to do? What am I going to do?" I would think of the kids and every cell would scream, I'm not done with my kids! I didn't tell them things that I need to tell them. O God, I'm not done yet! Then I would recall some of the awful things I had shouted at them in the past. O God, I owe them so many apologies.

I thought of Dan and felt such remorse. How many times we'd talked about getting away by ourselves and talking, without any time schedules or interruptions. I longed to recapture the closeness we once had. Why had we put it off? It hurt to scream so loud inside myself. It was shattering to think that nobody could hear it—not even God, I thought.

I don't recall how I got through the rest of the day. I don't remember the boys coming home from school. We must have eaten dinner. I must have switched to "automatic pilot." What I remember most vividly is the night, and all that happened inside me. The realization that there was not a single person to turn to, no one who could understand what I was going through, caused my inner world to crumble. Where were all the friends I thought I had? Why didn't they suspect I needed extra comfort and encouragement right now? Had I been such a phony that no one really missed me in my silence?

I paced the floor until well after midnight, asking myself questions, questions, questions. My soul longed to communicate with someone. My thoughts turned to God and I wanted to cry. I knew I couldn't get through this by myself, but did I dare call on God? I knew he was there, but it was as though I was afraid. I ached to call out to him. Help me, Lord! But I couldn't. I felt ashamed and I didn't know why—sort of like a little child who broke a window and was having to go tell the homeowner.

I sat in the moonlight near my living room window and recalled the night I'd lashed out at God. I said I'd never pray again. I had shaken my fist at him and said, "Who needs you?" I felt sorry now, but I didn't know how to reestablish a relationship with him. Would I have to beg to be forgiven? Should I offer to do something to earn his love? Would he help me after I'd been so nasty? Did he still love me after the way I'd closed the door on him?

I trembled at the realization that I had no choice. I knew he was there and he was the only one who could lift me from this place and give my life meaning. I rehearsed what I was going to say to him. I decided to sort of bargain by saying, "All right God, if you give me back my voice, I'll never say anything bad and I'll never criticize my children again. Only loving things will come out of my mouth, Lord." I wondered if I could keep a bargain like that. I decided not to pray that one.

I got up and walked around for awhile. Then I decided I needed to set up a "sanctuary" and get on with praying. I gathered some candles, a Bible, and a plaque with a picture of Jesus on it, and arranged them on the coffee table. In the back of my mind I knew I was just prolonging "getting on with it" by the rituals I was doing to get ready.

Something began to stir inside me and the time came when my soul couldn't wait any longer. I said, "O my God. O my God. O my God!" Tears streamed down my face. My body began to tremble, and sobs worked their way up from some place deep inside me. I crumbled to the floor and gripped the shag carpeting as waves of anguish flowed out of me. I had never cried so hard. I hadn't cried for thirty-five years. It seemed I was falling apart, never to be put back together again. I don't know how long I lay there, lost in my own pain.

There was no time in this realm, no awareness of the physical world, no phoniness, no intellectualizing, no cleverness. Just empty space, naked experience, and then—incredible awareness of the closeness of God. In that moment I knew he'd never left me. It was I who had gone from him.

I experienced God's forgiveness. I didn't have to grovel or plead for him to love me. He was enfolding and holding me in this desperate time. I felt such oneness with him as I poured out all those years' worth of tears, it was as though I was immersed in pure understanding.

I cried about the things happening and not happening in my life, about things that had happened prior to this time—in the inner city, and before that. My mind observed as my heart brought to my attention (and to God's) every hurtful or fearful thing that had happened in my life. As these experiences paraded through my consciousness, I was able to cry the tears that had waited so long for expression.

I told God that I didn't understand him. I'd felt rejected by him. I shared my doubts about having been led by him in my inner-city work. I cried about my marriage, my poor mothering, my feelings of inadequacy. It was as though I was watching the pages on a calendar turn backward through my entire life, recalling everything that had ever made me want to cry: experiences in high school, losing the spelling bee in third grade.

With each new outpouring of tears I felt an outflow of

energy until I was drained, spent, devoid of any power or strength. In the still space somewhere inside my hollowed-out being, a single thought winged its way. "Did I die?"

Tingles. I felt tingles in my hands, then in my feet. My heart began to beat noticeably faster as I admitted my excitement that I must still be alive.

With a sense of wonder and fascination, I experienced being filled with new life: something like warm honey flowing through every part of my body, liquid love being given in a transfusion, electric current coming into my body.

I had the desire to take a deep breath. When I inhaled, it was as though my muscles rejoiced in the peace that had come to them after what must have seemed a violent storm. Light. I felt filled with light, as if I was glowing. With my eyes closed, I could see myself filled with light, as if I was transparent. Light streamed out of every pore. I had such keen awareness in that moment of illuminated silence. I felt so alive, yet I wasn't moving. I felt so at one with God, and I wasn't even trying. I felt so at peace, and still none of my life's circumstances had changed. My mind felt uncluttered. There were no questions, no fears, no anger, no pain.

A prayer began to take form in my mind, a simple, brief, uncomplicated prayer. "God, what am I to do with my life?" I felt it flow out of me, Godward, without any anxiety or effort.

A moment after that prayer-question, a thought seemed to enter me instead of flow out of me. My soul knew it to be God. "I thought you gave your life to me."

I felt a little of my old argumentative spirit awaken as I mentally defended myself. "Lord, I did give myself to you. Remember at the retreat? Why do you think I went to the inner city? I was doing that for you. I did give myself to you, Lord."

"If you've given your life to me, then why have you taken it back?" That thought wasn't from me because I didn't even understand it. Had I taken my life back? My mind replayed my simple prayer, "What am I going to do with my life?" The words I and my seemed accentuated. I realized I had indeed taken responsibility for my life away from God. I longed for the relationship I'd once had with him. The trust that he would guide my life. The joy that came when we'd worked well together.

Everything seemed in slow motion. Gone was the frenzy, the panic I'd felt a few hours before. I decided to recommit myself to God. Suddenly I felt a shiver as I got in touch with some old childhood programming. The thought occurred to me, "What if I offer myself to God now, and he says, 'Who wants you? You can't do anything.' "

For a moment I again felt the terrible feelings I'd had of inadequacy and uselessness. I felt like a little girl who had a present to give to somebody but was afraid he'd look at it and say, "Never mind, you can keep it. I don't need it." Or a little girl who dropped the present on the way to a birthday party and couldn't find out if it was broken until it was opened. I really wanted to offer my gift to God but I was afraid it was broken and useless.

Very sheepishly I said, "Lord, I admit I've taken my life back and I'm so sorry. I see now that I had begun to run here and there, schedule things without first checking with you, plan and organize as though I were alone, receiving all the glory for my accomplishments myself. O Father, forgive me. I want to offer myself to you, Lord, for whatever purpose you might have for a mute in Garden Grove."

That night I gave God all of the concerns I had about my kids and husband and I felt that a thousand-pound weight was lifted from my shoulders. I gave him my future and any career I might have. I promised to serve and praise him in all that I did from that day on.

I felt heard. I was immersed in his love, baptized by the tears of many years. Out of the silence came a word: "Listen." I was not to understand its full significance until later. Right then I lay there and listened to the stillness, the night, the darkness.

I saw an image of a caterpillar crawling in the dirt, and then out on a limb. As though it were on a movie screen, I viewed a cocoon being formed. My heart fluttered as I realized the possible significance. I was in the cocoon of my life. I'd been in the dirt. I'd gone out on a limb. Now I was in a period when all seemed lost. I was like a prisoner—bound, restricted. The light had gone out of my life, just as it must seem to a caterpillar when it enters its temporary prison. I thought about what happens in a cocoon. The miraculous transformation. I got excited about the new creature that I was becoming as in my mind I saw a glorious butterfly emerge and take flight. I felt hope. O God, thank you for the joy I feel. Thank you for the hope I feel. Thank you for revealing your resurrection power to me through a caterpillar. Lord, I patiently await the time when my cocoon cracks open and I fly free in you.

I slowly got up from the floor, walked into the bedroom, crawled in bed, knowing that it had already happened. I had crawled into the arms of Jesus and was being rocked to sleep. Thank you, Lord.

The next morning I was awakened by my clock radio playing what seemed to be an unusually beautiful melody. I sat up and heard the boys in the kitchen (they had their own alarm clocks since Mother couldn't tell them any-more), and their chattering sounded like music to my ears.

Dan emerged from the bathroom and began to get dressed for work. I noticed how handsome he was. His words of greeting seemed so gentle and loving, and I realized in that moment how much I loved him and how long it had been since I'd let him know it. How foolish to think that since I couldn't say it aloud, I couldn't express it in other ways. I wondered why I hadn't thought of that before.

I looked out the window and noticed that the trees looked greener. Then I heard a bird sing. What a gorgeous day. Why was it so different . . . or was it?

For a while I honestly thought that everything around me had changed, but as the day progressed I knew for certain that it was I who had changed. I glided through the breakfast routine enjoying my children and their morning antics. There was tremendous optimism in me as I bid Dan and the boys goodbye as they went off to work and school.

I knew I was a new creature in Christ. This was the beginning of a new life.

CHAPTER 14

I walked through the house and wondered how it had
gotten so dirty. I had tremendous energy and was eager to
tackle long-neglected cleaning jobs. I hadn't felt like this
for months. It was as though I was plugged into an inex-
haustible source of power. I scrubbed, scoured, polished,
and danced to the music I heard in my mind. How can I
be so enthusiastic and not know what I'm enthusiastic
about?

As the day wore on, I pondered what had happened to
me the night before. I had experienced some magnificent
change. Where were the worry and fear of the future?
Where did the pain of the past go? It was as though my
life had been in black and white and suddenly it burst
into living color.

Many times since, I have tried to figure out what happened to me. One night I saw an image in my mind of a
jar of muddy water. It represented me. Over the years I
had allowed people to pour all sorts of things into me.
Opinions, ideas, information, prejudices, values, judg-
ments. Add those things to a million unexpressed feelings
and it all turns to bottled-up mud. I became afraid to share
anything that was in me for fear it would all come gushing
out. I was certain that if anyone saw the mud he would
never like me. So I was this jar of muddy water with the
lid screwed on tight.

I was to discover that the same lid that held the stuff inside kept me from being able to experience another person totally. The lid kept others from knowing me or loving me so that I could feel it.

As one might imagine, looking at the world through muddy water will distort everything. Hearing with mud in your ears makes for some strange messages and a lot of misunderstandings.

The more depressed I became with my throat problem, the weaker I felt—until I simply couldn't hold my lid on anymore. On that particular night, when I fell on my knees and cried out to God, my jar spilled. Out came all the contaminated water, right down to the sludge in my life. Out came everything that had been bottled up in me, everything that needed to be expressed, making room for God to pour in his Living Water. His fresh, clear, life-giving Water: Christ himself.

On this new morning I was able to see things as they really were, because the water in me was clear. I was beginning to see everything through the eyes of Christ and everything was beauty-full. The music I heard in everything, the love I heard in my family's voices, were because I was hearing without the distortion. I felt Love and I felt loved. Every time I think of it, I thank God for the experience of emptying myself that night so that he could fill me afresh with his Holy Spirit.

There was to be more silence, much time for meditating and contemplating, but it was a joyous time of rekindled love for God and my family. It was a time of hope. I constantly reminded myself that I was his, and that seemed to keep me from worrying. My faith seemed strong and I felt eager anticipation every day.

My third month of silence was unlike the first two months. This month was to become the most creative time in my life, a time of discovery and delight. I began to get acquainted with myself. To the degree, seemingly, that I could see and understand myself, I could empathize with and understand others. It was a wondrous time, when feelings became my friends as I learned to give them expression rather than keep them prisoner in my body.

Ideas began to bubble up. For the next few days after that special night my mind was filled with possibilities. It was like a water fountain with ideas being carried on sprays of sparkling clear water. Where had they all been before? Oh yes, down under the sludge.

One of the first things I realized was that I'd have to get back out among people. Something inside me knew I was created to be with people, working, sharing, serving. Initially, I would be embarrassed, but I would simply have to endure it until people got used to my silence. I remember praying, "Lord, I want my life to matter. I want to make a difference in the world—to give to it, not just take from it." In my heart I felt I had a lot to give, but I couldn't have named anything right then. I had love to give, but as yet I had no idea how to give it.

I began to venture out into the world again and to attend things. I returned to PTA and my church circle, my committees and our bowling league, our bridge club and my social clubs. I reentered all of those situations determined to get through the frustration of not being able to participate verbally.

It was a totally different experience for me. Now I was a spectator rather than an active participant. My pattern had always been to arrive early for a meeting, help set up, have a cup of coffee and chat with people as they arrived, organize things so the time together would run smoothly, and so on. Now I'd arrive as the meeting was starting so I could slip in unnoticed. I sat in the back so I could slip out without being questioned. I wanted to stay in the background since I couldn't contribute anything to the discussions or conversations. What a switch for a person who always before sat in the front row, had a comment for everything, and was always raising her hand.

I saw every one of those situations from a different perspective. Being in my old groups as a silent member was an experience that taught me many lessons.

As a constant spectator, I became a listener—not by choice but by default. I was surprised at what I began to notice as I focused my full attention on someone I thought I knew "like a book." I didn't really know the person at all. I learned that to really listen to someone you must give him or her your full attention (which I'd never been willing to do before). You must observe his body language, look at his facial expressions and hand motions, and, most important, try to *feel* his feelings. I'd never listened like that before because, when I had my voice, I was always rehearsing what I was going to say when someone was talking to me. I could hardly wait for the person to take a breath so I could interject *my* thoughts, ideas, opinions: what I'd read or seen on TV; whatever would build me up in the person's eyes.

Sensitivity to others was born in me at that time. I began to hear past the words that people were saying to what they were trying to say. I remember one person in particular in my PTA group who always talked. She retold the same stories until those around her wanted to climb the walls. We regarded her as someone we all had to put up with. I had spent time and energy trying to control her talking and thought I was handling the problem pretty well. Then during the time I was speechless I made a discovery.

At one of the meetings she began to yak the way she always did. As I watched, I felt a compassion for her that I'd never had. She must be lonely, I thought. She must feel that no one listens to her. I knew in that moment that this compulsive talker was crying out for love and acceptance. She wanted to be noticed and appreciated. She talked so much because no one was listening to her underlying message. She didn't realize how she was defeating herself, and everyone else seemed too busy to notice the destructive thing that was happening.

I made an effort to smile at her and to sit by her at meetings. I tried to look at her and let her know by my nodding and facial expressions that I was hearing what she was saying. She became quieter. She seemed a little more peaceful.

Another person in the group was a clown, always making jokes, puns, wisecracks. Many times she had bugged me. From my silent corner I studied her and sensed a hurting person. I suspected that she had a lot of pain in her life and that laughing was her choice over crying. I wrote a note to her asking her to tell me about herself, and she said, "My son has leukemia and I'm divorced. When my mother, who has arthritis, is well enough, I get to come to these meetings, because she can stay with Kevin." How could anyone have known that?

Other persons I'd been critical of when I could speak were all those who sat in the back rows and didn't actively participate. I used to think they must not be very bright or creative if they didn't contribute anything. I even wondered why they bothered to attend something if they didn't have opinions or ideas. Now I was one of those quiet people who sat in the back row and didn't speak. My mind was constantly spinning with ideas, but I couldn't express them. As I became one with these people, I wondered if they, too, had ideas and opinions—but for reasons, perhaps unknown even to themselves, simply couldn't get them out. Maybe they were afraid or had been hurt. Whatever the problem, I knew that they, too, were longing for love. Looking for understanding. Hoping for satisfying relationships.

The more I watched people, the more I heard. The more I heard and saw and sensed, the more I understood. The more I understood, the more I wanted to reach out to them. The more I wanted to reach out, the more frustrated I felt since I couldn't talk.

My desire to communicate with those around me was so great that I couldn't keep it inside. I simply had to find ways to express it. For a person who'd never been very affectionate (I hadn't come from a hugging family), for one who had never shown her feelings, it was frightening to try to think of ways to show my concern.

Not being a toucher or a hugger, I had always disguised my real message in code: "Do you want to go out to lunch?" I really wanted to say, "I really care about you." I'd say, "Hey, that's really neat," when what I wanted to say was, "I admire and respect you." I'd call a friend and say, "Do you have any coffee?" but I was really saying, "Hey, I really need to talk to someone."

I wasn't able to communicate even when I had a voice.

How on earth could I expect to without one? I set out to learn how to be more congruent. I wanted what I did on the outside to match what I felt on the inside. I knew it would involve my entire lifestyle and that I would have to learn to demonstrate my messages.

I'd have to begin by writing my thoughts and messages even though I'd had many shattering times with my little notes not being read or understood. I knew that quick jots would never suffice as a form of communication. I'd need to write at home, on all of the subjects that were important to me, and then find people to read them.

Boy, did I learn some things about myself! I hadn't realized how many hang-ups related to writing I had. My dread of writing showed up in my always being delinquent in letter writing, never making a grocery list even though Dan asked me to every week, not liking to write excuses for the boys if they missed school, etc.

In my silent meditations I traced this negative feeling about writing back to an experience in fifth grade. I was to write a report. I don't recall the subject, but I remember that ordinarily I copied something from a book, trying to reword it just enough to make the teacher think I'd understood what I was writing about. This time, however, I tried to write my own thoughts and feelings about the subject. I remember my excitement, thinking I had an understanding of what I was writing about. I put little philosophical comments in it, and I thought it was the best report I'd ever done. I carried it to school in a construction paper folder as if it were gold.

When I arrived in my classroom, I went to my seat and waited for a time when the teacher didn't seem too busy. I walked slowly up to her desk, placed the folder there, and returned to my seat. I watched her as she read it. I was nervous. Then, devastated, I saw her frown, pick up her red pencil, and begin to make circles and checks all over it. She must not like my ideas. I must really be dumb, I thought.

I see in retrospect that I made a decision that day in fifth grade. I would never write my feelings again. I would never risk having someone read them and judge them by the spelling, punctuation, and whether or not I made a capital letter in the right place. It had affected my whole life. I had avoided writing.

Now, however, since I had no voice, writing seemed the logical form of communication. Although it was hard to know where or how to start, I began. I wrote everything that came to mind. I poured out every thought, idea, and feeling on paper. I wrote about every emotion I could label. I wasn't writing for anyone to read, at first; I just wanted to get these things out of my body. It seemed that I could better understand and deal with things outside of myself than things inside. I wrote about frustrations, concerns, hopes, dreams, fears. I wrote prayers and even composed the answers I thought God would give. It was a beautiful release.

After several days of writing, I noticed that some of my thoughts had a rhythm to them, sort of like poetry. I'd written practically no poetry before, but this seemed to flow out of me and I was fascinated as though it came from someone else. Such a time of self-discovery. I read and reread my compositions and poetry and was amazed at what I was learning about myself. Sometimes while I was writing I would come upon a thought or feeling that I knew no words to describe. I could feel it but couldn't call it by a name. I would close my eyes to get in touch with the feeling, and sometimes a picture or color would come to my mind. One day Dan bought me a big box of oil pastels and I started to express some of my inner reactions with colors. I scribbled, colored, designed, and smeared magnificent colors. I had a freedom I'd never had before. It felt so good to know that no one was going to grade it or ask, "What's that?"

Excitement rose inside me with each discovery, each expression. The hope that I could accomplish something in my life was being restored. It even occurred to me that some people communicate through music and, although I'd always loved music, I was not a musician. During those days I would find myself sitting down at the piano and plunking out a tune I was hearing in my head. Much to my surprise, I began to combine my poetry with music. I came to realize that, not only could I be a writer, I could be an artist, poet, composer. I never knew that these abilities were inside me, but they must have been there all my life. It seemed amazing I'd never discovered them before.

I realized the power of negative reinforcement, since I could see that that was the reason I had never tried these things after I got out of school. By that time I was pretty convinced that I was incapable and had no talent. When everyone around you says that something you've done is no good, you soon start to believe them because they're the judges. As a child, I felt smart, but no one else seemed to think so. I decided I must not be. Now, without the judges present, I was experiencing the joy of expressing myself and was loving every minute of it. It was as if every day was Christmas and I was finding gifts within myself and getting to open them one at a time.

So, my third month of silence was filled with the wonder of writing, music, art, and sculpting, and became the most creative time of my life. It was such a contrast to the other two months. I began to make items for our church's bazaar, which gave me a sense of contributing. When I wasn't home doing something creative, I was attending something and trying to listen creatively.

Every so often I would think about my experience with God that night. I would wonder what he meant by "Listen," but maybe that's what I was doing. I was listening to myself and to those around me in a completely new way.

PART THREE
The Ungame®

CHAPTER 15

Day in and day out I listened to conversations: between husbands and wives, parents and kids, teens and friends, committee members, brothers and sisters, and I became increasingly horrified with what I was hearing. I no longer heard only the words. I now seemed able to hear *past* the words to people's trapped feelings.

I would come home from a meeting or social gathering with conversations being replayed over and over in my mind. I heard the echoes of a conversation between a couple we played bridge with. The wife had tried to share a feeling and the husband had reacted to her words and missed the point. He couldn't be blamed, though, because she had disguised her feeling by making a statement that made him feel a need to defend himself. She said, "Jim, we never do anything anymore." (I suspected she was wanting to say, "I miss having your undivided attention.")

His reaction was to point out to her all the things they'd done together in the past month: grocery shopping, attending church, visiting her aunt, etc. He then reminded her that at that very moment they were playing bridge together and it was her bid. The rest of the people laughed, and I watched her crawl into a shell for the rest of the evening.

I grieved when I recalled a little four-year-old who wandered into the living room saying he'd heard a noise and couldn't sleep. He was told, "You'd better disappear before I blister your bottom!" I watched his little lower lip tremble as he hung his head and walked down the long hall alone. I wondered if he really wanted to say he was afraid, but had already learned that "big boys are sup-posed to be brave." So he made a statement that was not even heard. On top of his fear he now had to add the humiliation of hearing the adults laugh as his parent threatened him.

As I recalled such vignettes I realized that everyone seemed to be talking in code and no one was taking time or had skills to decode the messages. Someone would say some words and someone else would react to those words. They're not saying what they mean or meaning what they say! How can anyone communicate that way?

I made a startling discovery about myself that night as I faced the fact that I was just like the people I was watch-ing and listening to. I searched myself for clues as to how I got that way and how I could change. The discovery was that all my life I'd had a sarcastic sense of humor. I could cut somebody down in a flash with a few words and have everyone else laughing at the same time. I had felt power-ful with that ability and had used it since high school. I could see how I'd used it recently with my husband and kids.

But why did I do it? Why did I always have to get a laugh even at the expense of another person? I could see how I even set up situations to slay someone in the presence of an audience. (I was not sarcastic or joking when talking to one person, but just when I had an audience.) I did a replay of some of those times in my life and could see now that, at those moments, I had been hurt or embarrassed or threatened. But I couldn't let anyone know, so I was like a wounded animal that snapped at those around me.

I didn't like looking back at those incidents but they gave me insights, not only into myself but into those I came in contact with every day. I began to see that every-one was probably hurting to some degree—was perhaps lonely, frustrated, feeling inadequate, but feeling the need to pretend that he or she had it all together and was doing great.

I prayed an ardent prayer that night. "Dear God, how can I help people communicate more effectively? How can I help people get in touch with feelings that have been bottled up for years? How can I help others get feelings out of their body so they don't cause ailments? Lord, how can I help people break the codes? Or not have to speak in codes anymore? O God, help me to help them."

I longed to find a way to share what I was learning with someone. I dreamed of getting some friends together and going over all the data I was gathering. What if some people got together and tried to be totally honest and shared themselves? "O God, give me some clues as to how I can make that happen . . ." I fell asleep.

In the days to come I began to notice how differently I was acting toward my children. It was such a contrast to the first month, when I wanted to grab them and shake them, and the second month, when I almost didn't care if they existed. I watched and listened to them with a sense of wonder, and I had so much more patience than I'd had before. Because I was calm, I was able to hear more of what they were saying and, lo and behold! I started to be able to hear beyond *their* codes.

One day my son came home from school and barged through the front door. I looked up from my rocking chair in time to see the glass shake in the window. He threw his lunch box down, stomped his foot, and screamed, "I hate school! I'm never going back! My teacher's mean!" With that he stormed to his room and slammed the door with such force that the entire house rattled.

Had I been able to talk, my reaction probably would have been something like this. First, I would have yelled at him for throwing the door open and hitting the wall. Then I would have reminded him of the glass in it (all of which he knew and had been reminded of 100 times). I would have then screamed about the lunch box that cost six dollars, and belittled him by saying, "Don't you know that that thermos is breakable?" When he stomped to his room, I would have said, "Now you quit acting like that or

you're not going to go to the park!'' When he said he
didn't like his teacher, I probably would have said, "Why,
your teacher is a lovely woman. I met her last week at
PTA . . ." More than likely, I would have gone down the
hall and hollered through his closed door, "And you are
too going back to school, if I have to take you there
myself!"

That's the way I used to react to my kids when they got
mad or threw tantrums. You see, for some reason I
couldn't tolerate their getting angry. It triggered such anger
in me that I usually sent them to their room with some
sarcastic remark and several threats.

Thank God I couldn't talk. I learned a priceless lesson
about decoding my son's messages that day. Because my
old patterns of behavior were being broken, I had to find a
new way to react to that kind of outburst.

My first sensation was one of shock. Then I felt anger at
his harsh words and his banging the door against the wall.
I was furious when he threw the lunch box. And I must
admit that when he left the room, still yelling, the thought
of strangling him entered my mind. Because I didn't know
how to express my reactions when things were happening
so fast, I just sat and stared. Immobilized. After pacing
around for a few minutes, I collapsed on the couch, baffled as to how to handle such behavior. I couldn't just
ignore it.

While I was searching for some calculated reaction, he
reappeared, looking sober. He slowly walked over and sat
down next to me, and in two minutes he had his head
buried in my lap. Like a volcanic eruption, he began to
cry. "Mom, it was so awful, The kids all laughed when I
gave my report. I was so embarrassed!" Since I couldn't
speak, I put my arm around him—which I wouldn't nor-
mally have done because we would have been yelling at
each other. He went on, "My teacher said I didn't study,
and I did." Then the story he had tried to tell in code
began to emerge. He had gotten up to give a report he'd
worked on way into the night before. He mispronounced a
word and the teacher corrected him. He mispronounced it
again and the kids laughed. He got nervous and forgot a

whole section. The teacher then told him to start over and there was that dumb word again. This time the class howled and the teacher told him to sit down. He felt shattered and cried, and of course the kids teased him. I felt the pain the little guy was feeling. Tears came to my eyes as I lived through his tale of woe with him.

Of course he would have to code that message. I had never allowed him to show or share his feelings. I had been doing the very thing that people had done to me. Saying things like, "Don't be a baby! Big boys don't cry! What a scaredy-cat! That couldn't have possibly hurt! What a sissy! That shouldn't bother you!" On and on. . .

I hadn't allowed my boys to express any negative feelings (I was the judge). So why was I surprised that they learned to code their messages? Thank goodness, now I wasn't able to talk him out of any of those feelings. Now he could trust me with the real stuff. I watched a miracle occur right before my eyes. As soon as he finished his account, he looked up, saw my tears, sat up tall, and said, "Can I have a cookie?" We hugged and he trotted off. I had never seen him recover from anything so quickly.

My ability to decode improved with each day and before long I could interpret almost any message in a second. For example, when my other son said, "I hate Bobby. I'm never going to play with him again!" I heard that he was angry at Bobby. I patted him as he told me what had happened. Bobby had invited him to go somewhere. My son got ready and went out to the curb to wait. When Bobby and his mother drove by, it was obvious that Bobby had taken someone else. (I found out later that his mother had said, "You can bring one friend," and he had invited two.) I could feel my little boy's heartbreak and feeling of rejection.

Questions often drive kids away. Questions like, "What happened? What were you doing there? Why didn't you tell him . . . ? How many times have I told you . . . ?" Now I was finding I got all the information without asking a thing if I showed genuine interest and touched or held the boys. Thank you, Father.

My most profound experience of truly listening occurred

when a young girl came to my house and pounded on the door for five solid minutes. I didn't always answer the door when I was home alone, since I never figured out how to handle kids, or salesmen, or someone selling their religion. When I finally opened the door I saw a forlorn young woman whom I'd met only once. She was sobbing.

My first thought was, "Does she know I can't talk?" A wave of inadequacy swept through me as I tried to gesture to her that I was unable to speak, but she didn't even notice my hands waving around or my pointing. She stumbled in and went to the kitchen, where she collapsed at the table and continued crying. I didn't know what to do, so I just walked around the kitchen and looked at her as she slumped over. I wasn't used to being around someone crying. I always felt so awkward if a person even got choked up, and I would do everything to change the subject, make them laugh, or pretend I didn't notice. None of those old patterns seemed like options in this case. What can I do? O God, she's hurting. Lord, what can I do?

She eventually began to blubber out her story. "My dad kicked me out of the house. I hate my dad, he doesn't understand." She said it with such emotion that I felt what she was feeling in every cell of my body. She went on to say she'd been kicked out because her dad found out that she was pregnant. Her dad hated the boyfriend and had warned her that if she continued to see him she'd have to move. "I don't have any place to go," she sobbed.

I tried to imagine what it would be like to be pregnant, unmarried, and have no place to go. I felt heavy with grief for her and wanted somehow to let her know. "Touch her," I said to myself. Why did that seem so hard? I never touched people. Still, it was the only way to get some people's attention if I needed to act something out. I remember looking at my hand and wondering why it felt like lead, why it didn't want to move. My mind said, "Do it! Do it!" but my body said, "I'm not used to this. What will she think? What if she pulls away?" My mind won over my body, and with my left hand I reached over to my right hand, lifted it, and put it on her shoulder. I felt like a robot acting at the command of my "higher self."

The most amazing calm came over her in the next few minutes as I just patted her. Her story continued with the painful discovery that her boyfriend now loved someone else and had broken up with her. She twisted and writhed as she told of the love and trust she'd had in him. How I felt the pain of that lost love. My tears begin to flow as I shifted from feeling the anger about her father to the grief of her loss. Her world had collapsed, it seemed—but there was still more. Word of her pregnancy had spread through the place where she worked, and her boss had called her in and fired her from the only job she'd ever had. She had pleaded with him to allow her to stay since she would have to get an apartment, but he hadn't been persuaded. Then she'd backed her car into a parked van in a parking lot, and, because she had let her insurance expire, she left the scene without reporting it. Now she was terrified of being caught.

I had never heard so many traumatic things come out of anyone's mouth at one time. Probably I had never listened to someone's whole story before. Another realization about myself. Had I had my voice, I would have done as I always did. At the end of their first sentence, I would start making suggestions, or wisecracks. Or I would use their opening line as a kickoff for one of my stories, making it big and dramatic so they would think theirs was little in comparison.

What a sickening discovery. How many times had I said to someone, "Oh, don't worry about it, it'll be better tomorrow," or "So who needs him?" "Tell him where to get off!" "You can find another job. There are lots of things available." How awful I'd been to people! I had never responded to their feelings. I hadn't even fully heard their complaints. My whole lifestyle was designed to shove feelings back and to act as if I never had them.

Here I was, allowing someone to get her entire painful experience out of her, and, much to my amazement, I was feeling what she was feeling. I continued to pat her as she went on unloading everything that came to mind. For the first time in my life I felt comfortable crying with some-one.

She must have known I was listening, although at times she was so into her story that she seemed oblivious to my presence. Finally it was finished. She stopped crying and shaking. She looked up at me for the first time and I'm sure she noticed that my cheeks were wet with unwiped tears. I jumped to my feet, grabbed a box of Kleenex, offered her one, and we both laughed (hers was aloud, mine inside myself). I felt led to offer her a cup of coffee, so I went to the stove and pointed to the coffee and also to my cup rack. She said, "Oh, I'd love one." As we looked at each other and smiled, I didn't realize I was witnessing a transformation of a human being.

I was to spend hours pondering and meditating on that experience in the coming months, searching for the secret of it. While it was happening, however, I was unaware of the impact it would have on my future. It was like watching a flower unfold, not really able to see it happening, but suddenly aware that it had. Her eyes were so bright and clear and there was a sparkle that hadn't been there when she arrived. A rainbow. What was the difference? Nothing had changed. The problems were still there. What is this peace we both seem to feel? Why the smiles?

Suddenly she said, "I suppose I could call _____ and ask if I could stay there a few days. I could probably get a job at _____. Hey, and I could ride the bus there! I could baby-sit my sister's kids and start saving my money . . ."

She began to talk faster, getting more excited with each possibility. To my amazement I realized that these thoughts were not coming from outside sources, they were coming from inside her. Soon she was standing up and saying, "Yeah, if I did _____, then _____ would probably happen and then I could call _____." Her arms were flying in every direction as she enthusiastically dramatized the possibilities.

My heart raced as though I were skiing down a mountain. I tried to show her how thrilled I was that ideas were coming to her, so I did everything I could to show it with my body and expressions and hands. We were both kind of dancing around the kitchen when all of a sudden she stopped. She looked directly at me for a second and then, like a rush of wind, threw her arms around me. "Oh,

Rhea, thank you, thank you, thank you." I had never been
hugged so tightly nor so sincerely. What had I done? What
on earth had I done, I thought? I had never been thanked
like that for any advice I ever gave! She stepped back with
a radiant smile on her face. "I'll let you know how it all
turns out," she said as she ran out the front door.

I was stunned as I watched her briskly leap over the
shrubs surrounding the yard. She was gone. What had
happened? Lord, what transformed that girl—yes, from a
caterpillar to a butterfly? Dear God, help me to understand
how it happens so I can bring it about *intentionally* rather
than just by accident. Lord, is this what you mean by
"listening"? Am I doing it? I want this to happen in *all* of
my relationships."

More than anything in my life, I wanted to be able to
facilitate that kind of life-changing. It became my dream
and my prayer in the days to come. As I relived such
experiences I began to get clues. The first clue was the
similarity of what happened to her and what happened to
me that night with God. That pouring-out of all the darkness and getting right down to the sludge of life in the
bottom of the jar. Having it heard and accepted, not dis-
cussed or challenged or criticized. No advice was given.

In an atmosphere of love, all that darkness was simply
allowed to come out, and it was felt by someone else. I
had experienced it with God that night and now she had
experienced it with me. God had not responded to me
with any lectures, sermons, or Scripture quotes. I had felt
wrapped in his love, completely forgiven, accepted in his
presence. Love seemed to fill the space inside me with
hope and joy. I got in touch with a stream of creative
ideas. Possibilities. As though I had struck oil.

The ideas that came to her were evidently buried inside
her under the sludge of her life. When she shoveled the
sludge out, those possibilities were uncovered.

The Holy Spirit had worked through me. I began to
wonder if problems and solutions came in matched sets.
Maybe we can't get in touch with our own solutions
because they get covered up by so many people's advice
and suggestions that they're buried. When we lose contact

with the part of us that "knows," that creative part, we feel inadequate and insecure. This kind of listening could free people from the prisons that are built by us—first as a hiding place, but then becoming the only place in which we know how to function.

Look at what had happened in my life. I had built a prison around me and then sat inside wondering why I had no visitors. O God, help me to take the walls of my prison down so I can be available to haul away the debris of someone else's life. I knew I couldn't take anyone else's walls down, but I could wait outside, loving and encouraging someone while he did it.

Maybe I can become a professional "listener," I thought. Maybe that's how God is going to use my life. I had listened to that young girl with my whole being, not just with my physical ears. Maybe that's what is meant when people talk about listening with the heart. The word *heart* has the word *ear* right in the center; also the word *hear*. On that occasion my mind was not filled with rehearsing, planning, staging, or worrying about how I would come across. The result was that she and I felt a communion, a closeness. She knew it and she felt freed.

CHAPTER 16

My head seemed full of discoveries and insights. My heart felt tender and committed to finding some way to help people communicate. My body still felt energized even though it had been three weeks since my new beginning.

One night I prayed, "Dear God, help me to find some way to use the things I'm learning, so I can help other people. Help me to pull together the bits and pieces of wisdom and truth and to put them into a form that can communicate. Lord, I need a way to reach out and touch the hurting people in the world. Speak to me tonight. Express through me tonight. O Father, show me how I might love in a way that heals others. Amen."

I sat there at my kitchen table, pencil in hand, and waited for the Spirit to guide me. I had a large sketch pad in front of me, as I often did while I was thinking. I was in the habit of doodling as ideas came to me. Sometimes I would draw or make designs, other times I would write words or music.

On this night, I found myself thinking about all the persons I'd had meaningful conversations with during the past few weeks. I saw an image in my mind of them walking along a path going up a mountain. They were all on the same path, but each on a different part of the path. There were beautiful meadows and sparkling streams along portions of the path, but I could also see hazardous places: cliffs, bramble bushes, slippery rocks, and the like. In order to get to the top of the mountain, each would have to pass through the various areas, but perhaps at different times. I could see other paths also, but they, too, made their way through a variety of terrains.

Because people were spread out, they were each experiencing the area they were in, alone, not knowing that someone had been there before them and that someone would be coming into the place after they had passed through. It occurred to me that maybe we are at different places in our lives from those around us. Perhaps that's why it's hard to find relationships or companionship at the deeper levels of our lives. Oh, if we could just tarry for awhile at one of the resting places and be willing to share with someone else who comes along, letting that person know that we, too, have experienced fear in those dangerous places, and anxiety and doubt in the dark places. If we could let another know that we get angry with ourselves when we stumble or lose our way. Maybe we could give encouragement to one who is tiring or wanting to give up in despair.

How comforting it would be if we knew we could talk to someone who'd experienced something that we have yet to go through; it would prepare us and confirm that we are not alone. People's experiences aren't *that* unique.

We see others along the trail and assume they have it all together. We think they don't have any problems, that they have it made. We think, "How could they ever understand *my* problem?" I remember thinking so many times in my life that I had it harder than anyone else and that God must not love me as much. Now in my mind I could see that nobody had it made when it came to having to go through trials and feelings like fear, grief, loneliness, frustration, anger, and so on. Yet people reacted in many different ways to the same obstacle. What made the difference?

As I was thinking about these things, I began to sketch a road around the border of the large tablet. I thought of it as the Road of Life. Next I drew things along the road to

symbolize some of the feelings one might have on the
Road of Life. I wrote Happy Times, Sad Times, Excited
Times, Depressed Times. There were places for loneliness,
fear, joy, love, grief, pride. I drew little way-stations along
the road to represent the times when there doesn't seem to
be any particular problem or feeling.

Could I ever get a group of people together to talk about
where they are (and have been) on their path? I felt
ecstatic at the thought until I realized that it wouldn't be
easy. Why did I think they would talk about feelings when
they may never have expressed them before?

My hands kept working as though they were not connected to my mind, adding things here and there. I was
watching my hands create something that I had to ponder
in order to understand. Some of it I didn't understand.
The road went around the board and connected so that it
was unending. The thought came to me that we don't go
through these areas only once in our life, but many times.
Each time is different, depending on other circumstances
and perhaps because we have a deeper level of understanding.

I began to think of some of my friends. Where were they
on the road? Were some of them going through a tough
time? Were some of them depressed or afraid? I wanted to
ask them.

In my mind I saw a group of my friends sitting around
the table with my tablet lying in the center. All I had to do
was get them to talk. I watched on my imaginary movie
screen as I invited them to share their feelings about
where they were in life. None of them would. I was
baffled, and still I knew that people weren't apt to do it
just because someone asked them to. I asked them why
they didn't want to share at that level and they all answered at the same time by calling out words and phrases.
I heard the word *criticism* and *put-down*. I heard "fear of
being laughed at," "fear of sarcasm," "belittling." I heard
that they didn't want "advice" or a "lecture." They didn't
want to be challenged or have to defend themselves. They
wanted no joking.

As those words tumbled into my consciousness, I realized that they were the reasons I'd never shared what was inside me. The reason people could now share such things with me was because I couldn't do any of those things to them. I can't describe the feeling of elation I had when that all clicked!

Then I thought, "How can I see to it that no one experiences those painful things?" I had no sooner posed the question than the answer came. Don't allow anyone to talk except to tell about himself. That would do it, I thought. I wondered if I could get a group of people to promise to be silent while others talked about their life experiences and ideas. If they would be willing to do it, they might discover how different that kind of listening is. Maybe they, too, would hear beyond the words to real meanings.

I saw my hand write across the tablet, "everyone must be silent except on his own turn." Turn? I hadn't thought about turns. But the minute I said "turns" in my mind I could see that there would need to be turn-taking. In a flash I saw a re-creation of so many meetings I'd been to where everyone spoke (shouted?) at once. In almost every social situation I was in, I could predict who would do all the talking and who would sit quietly on the sidelines. If people took turns, it would mean that the gregarious, talkative person would have to simmer down, so that the shy, quiet person could talk without the fear of being interrupted or ignored. Nobody could monopolize. It would be more equal.

I closed my eyes and imagined the group promising to take turns sharing while remaining silent between turns as they listened. Then I saw another pitfall. People began to talk about grocery prices, baseball scores, politics, fashions, their children. There's nothing wrong with those subjects; they can be fun to share, but I found in my own life that they're a lot more enjoyable after the pain is gone. They can be hell to listen to when you're hurting.

The vision seemed to continue. I marked the road off so that dice could determine which area a person would talk about. I still wasn't certain how I could keep the group on the subject of feelings. Yet that kind of openness seemed to be a key to wholeness and more fulfilling relationships.

After awhile I put the drawing aside but the scene continued in my mind as I took a small tablet and relaxed in the living room. I began to think of questions that might help people to share some of their inner self. Once I started to write them down, they just bubbled out. Some of them were questions I had wanted to ask someone. Others were questions I wished someone would ask me—and wait long enough for me to write my answer. Questions poured out of me long into the night, until I had nearly 100 on many different subjects. One that I imagined my husband answering was, "How would you describe the perfect wife?" Another was, "Do you ever feel lonely?" I wondered how he would answer.

What four things are most important in your life?
How would you define love?
Share a turning point in your life.
What do you want to be doing in ten years?
Share a time when your feelings were hurt.
If you were told you had only one week to live, how would you spend it?
What is something that makes you angry?
Share something that you fear.
If you could hang a motto or saying in every home in the world, what would it be?
Give three words to describe how you feel right now.

I wrote several questions pertaining to childhood because I was discovering how connected we are to the child we once were. I am the sum total of every experience I had when I was little and, although my childhood was 100 times better than some, I still managed to get bumped, bruised, and scarred emotionally. In more recent years I have found the tremendous value of sharing about those little (or big) childhood traumas with someone. Each time I recall and share a little more, I get rid of more of the sediment in the bottom of my jar. I feel a bit more whole. And after I've shared with someone about a painful childhood time, my response to things happening is different, and so is the degree of pain or sadness.

At some point that night I felt emptied and decided to go to bed. I placed the little tablet with the questions on the big tablet with the road. Somehow I felt complete. Something was finished. I didn't understand what had happened. Would I ever be able to find anyone to sit around my drawing and answer my questions? Maybe I would ask my family. Maybe I'll just wait and see . . . I drifted off to sleep.

As I look back to that night I wonder if I would have believed it if someone had walked into my kitchen and said, "Rhea, those scribbles are going to change millions of people." More than likely I would have thought to myself, "No way! I could never do anything that big! Besides I might be a mute."

It was as though I had given birth to a child. I had conceived an idea, gone through a gestation period, experienced the labor, and given birth. The next morning as I looked at it lying on the kitchen table I experienced a sense of wonder similar to that of seeing my newborn sons. No one knows whether a newborn will be healthy or sickly, or what it's going to do with its life. I had no idea what was to come of this creation. I carried it into the living room and put it on a coffee table to make room for breakfast. It had come "through" me but did not seem to be "of" me.

A day went by before my family questioned it. They were used to seeing my artwork, scribbles, "interesting" clay sculptures, and wooden plaques, so they didn't always question things. The fact that I couldn't answer probably had something to do with it too. Eventually, however, someone asked what it was. I grabbed my pencil and pad and wrote, "I think it's a game." My family offered to try it out that evening and I felt nervous. I found six spools in my sewing basket to use for markers and borrowed dice from another game.

That evening we sat around a table and experienced my creation. More than that, we experienced each other as we played together. It seemed incredible, but we learned more about each other in one hour than we'd learned in five years. Or maybe since the beginning of time. We had a marvelous time talking about things that had never come up in our conversations before. Things we were feeling or going through. Dreams we had. Our hopes for the future, and so on. One brother sighed after a turn and said he was so relieved that the other brother hadn't laughed at what he said. Daddy shared some fears he had about losing his job and we were surprised.

Finally, finally, I could write about the things going on inside me and someone would wait until I finished. I could roll the dice, move my marker, draw a card, show everyone what it said, write my answer on a tablet, and show them what it said. They cared. They were surprised at my being so lonely. It felt good to let them know I had feared having cancer or that I was dying.

The night I drew the game, I had marked off the road on the tablet (which I'll now call the game board) in two-inch sections. The next day I decided to color it and draw little pictures around the road. I made the squares different colors.

As we began to play that night, drawing a card on our turn, it occurred to me that since we had all promised to remain silent, we needed a turn occasionally when we could let off steam. Not only was it difficult to keep our mouths shut when we heard an opinion or feeling, but we found that after you have heard so many ideas from several people, your mind begins to spin with things you want to say. Then you're no longer able to listen as well.

Since I had used three colors on the road, we decided that on the red spaces we'd draw a card. We called that space "Tell It Like It Is." If we landed on a blue space we would be free to say anything on our mind, on any subject. We called those spaces, "Do Your Own Thing." That way people could empty their heads so they could listen again. We used the Do Your Own Thing space to ask any questions we had about what someone said, or to say comforting things to someone if they had shared something that made them feel vulnerable or raw.

I had left some white spaces on the board and we called those "Hang-Ups." On each of those was a word like fear, worry, jealousy, complaining, impatience, etc. If someone landed there he had to tell whether or not that particular thing was his hang-up at that time. Later we decided that the Hang-Up spaces could be a "nonverbal" turn. If you related to the word on the space you could move your marker to a corresponding place on the board without needing to explain. If someone was curious about what you worried about or feared, or whatever, he could ask on a Do Your Own Thing space. So there were three different ways a person could share as he or she moved around the little Road of Life, each offering an opportunity to reveal more of who he or she is.

I remember some of the responses on that first night we played. I had included some lighthearted questions in the "deck" so that the experience would be fun as well as informative, but I had no way of anticipating how someone would answer.

Dan and I were shocked with an answer one of the boys gave to the question, "If you could have two famous people for parents, whom would you choose?" He thought for about five seconds and said, "Abraham Lincoln for my dad and Raquel Welch for my mother." Dan and I looked at each other with big eyes. It was hard not to question that right then, but because we'd promised not to talk except on our turn, we stayed quiet. It seemed to take forever for one of us to get a Do Your Own Thing so we could ask him why those two. I found myself fantasizing a scene with Abe doing the yard work while Raquel cooked dinner. I was so caught up in the daydream that I almost missed Dan's asking him when he finally landed on the appropriate space. The boy's answer: "Well, we're studying Abraham Lincoln in class and I like him, and the teen-agers always talk about Raquel, so I thought it would be neat to say she was my mother!" We breathed a sigh of relief. For a moment we feared our little boy had grown up without our noticing it.

We had some laughs as we played that night, and we had some tears. There were several startling revelations. One in particular was when our ten-year-old drew the question, "What do you want to be doing in ten years?"

He read it aloud and sat there staring for a moment. He flipped the card back onto the table, leaned back in his chair, and said, "Ah, forget it! I'll be dead!" I was shocked. Why would my son say that so matter-of-factly? A few turns later someone could ask him about it. His response: "Well, when I'm eighteen I'll have to go to the Viet Nam war and I'll probably get killed." With that, he pushed back from the table and walked away with his head down.

I had never realized that my children walked around with that cloud over their life. It was true the Viet Nam war was raging and had been for as long as they could remember. And of course, it was on the news every time you turned on the television. Yes, it was a part of my son's life. It gave me insights into his lack of enthusiasm about life. It must be very hard (if not impossible) for a kid to care whether his room is straight, his hair combed, his fingernails clean, his shirt matching his socks, his bike brought in, or his allowance saved. How could he have any incentive to do anything if he thought he was going to live only ten more years?

We were to explore this for weeks and it was good. I was glad to be in touch with my boys' fears and concerns. It enabled me to comfort them, but most important to listen to them. After his feelings came out and were heard, my son was able to hear our thoughts about the possibility that the war wouldn't go on forever. For a child who had never known peace, that was new to him. And even if it did, he wouldn't necessarily have to participate. Just hearing us say that seemed to relieve his mind. We saw positive changes in his attitudes, schoolwork, and happiness. How thankful we were to have uncovered that fear, so that he could express it and be comforted.

CHAPTER 17

What a wonderful time our family had talking to one
another with my little homemade game. We christened it
"Tell It Like It Is," since that phrase was popular, and it
seemed best to describe what happened.

A few days after our family had tried out Tell It Like It
Is, we had guests come to our home for an evening. Since I
was unable to talk, we had done almost no entertaining.
People seemed to feel uncomfortable around me since
two-way conversations weren't possible. Most people
would ask questions and then become embarrassed because they couldn't think of anything to say when I
couldn't answer. Often I was exhausted after guests left,
from having to play charades all evening. On this particular night Dan began the evening by saying, "Why don't we
play this little game Rhea made? We had a great time with
it the other night." The other couple was agreeable and we
had a wonderful time for over two hours.

We had known those friends for years, but we found we
didn't really know them. We had played bridge with them,
bowled with them, and had hours of enjoyable times, but
we never knew what was going on inside them. We
laughed hard and shared some of their pain. One of them
was able to squeeze my arm and say, "I'm sorry I haven't
been a better friend while you're going through this throat

thing. I just haven't known what to do." That felt so good to me: to have someone say it out loud rather than act as if it would never occur to her that I might miss my friends.

After our beautiful experience together, the couple asked if they could borrow the game so they could play it with their teen-agers. They went out the door marveling at things they'd learned about each other. The last thing I heard as they walked to the curb was, "We've been married twenty-two years. How come I didn't know *that* about you?" They both laughed as they got in their car. I could hardly wait to hear how it went with their teens whom they described as very quiet.

It was two days before my friend came to my door to report on their experience. Both of the kids agreed to play for half an hour, if they could quit then. The parents said OK, so they began. It was the first time in over a year that the four of them had sat down together, let alone said anything meaningful to each other. My friend described some of the things that took place. The father had been able to confess his feeling of inadequacy in knowing how to talk to or help his kids. Everyone listened. On the next turn the daughter got a card that said, "Name someone you respect and tell why." She immediately said, "My dad, because he's the most honest and generous man I know." There was a warm feeling in the group as the younger son was able to share how much he hated being compared to his older sister, and how he always felt put down by her comments. She reached over, touched him, and said, "I'm sorry." Everyone promised to try to be more sensitive to that in the future, and after an hour and a half they put it away and all hugged each other for the first time in years.

As she was telling me all this, I looked to see if she had the game with her. "I hope you don't mind," she said, "but my daughter took it to school yesterday where they played it in one of her classes, and tonight she wants to take it to her youth group. She promises to bring it to you tomorrow. Oh, by the way, her teacher would like for you to make five copies for her classroom and I would like two or three to give as gifts."

I was so excited that I danced around right there in front of her. Then it hit me. Seven or eight games? That one took me all night to make. I couldn't imagine how I'd ever get them done, but I nodded my head.

When her daughter returned the game the next day, she told me that what she liked best about it was that she could say something to her folks and not get a lecture or a lot of advice in return. Also, she could hear her parents say something without feeling defensive or blamed. "It's neat," she said as she turned to go. "I'll probably need to borrow it again."

I had my assignment—eight games. I didn't like to call it a game, though, because it wasn't a game. Games are competitive, and this experience isn't. In games you play to win. In this, you play for the joy of playing. Games are usually "pretend," like you're buying property, solving a murder, or the like, and in Tell It Like It Is, it's just the opposite. You don't pretend; you try to be real. Still, it did have a board, markers, dice, and a deck of cards, all the ingredients of a standard game. I called it a game because there wasn't a word to describe it.

In the coming days I was very busy drawing roads, typing questions on recipe cards, coloring pictures, writing captions, composing rules. All the while I was praising God for what I could see happening in people's lives as a result of this simple tool. "O dear Lord, thank you, thank you. This is changing lives already. Lord, how can it be? Is this what you want me to do? I'll keep doing it until you let me know otherwise. OK, Lord? Thank you for the joy I feel as I make these games. Amen."

What a thrill to deliver those eight games with their pretty colored spools and each drawn on a different color of poster paper. Those first games were like seeds planted by a stream of living water, each to bear fruit in due season. The fruit would contain seeds that would be sown, and there would be more fruit, which meant more requests for games. Many more.

I was to spend many many hours at my kitchen table creating duplicates of my original. I began to get orders in the mail, and with each order there was always a note telling about an experience that someone had had. My heart would sing. What a wonderful feeling, to know that God is using you. Thank you, Father, for choosing me.

Every day was filled with excitement, as I got up and made a new game for some new person. At some point I realized I would be able to reach more people this way than I had ever reached talking. Of course, I had no idea how far these little games were going to spread. With each home delivery I gained a little more self-esteem and confidence that I could matter. I felt hopeful. When I worked in the inner city, I had discovered how important hope was. I knew it for certain, now, because in my own life, when I didn't have hope, I didn't care about anything. I had no incentive even to try. Thank you, God, for hope.

One day I saw on my calendar that it was the twenty-ninth day. Tomorrow I had an appointment with the doctor. I couldn't believe how fast the time had gone, compared with the other months. As I was coloring one of my gameboards, I thought, "You know, if I go to the doctor tomorrow and he tells me I'm going to be a mute, I think I'll be able to handle it." I had discovered that, if I was open, God could use me and work through me in ways I never would have imagined. I had been finding someone to play the game with every day and, because of that, my mind stayed clear and empty of worry and concern. There were no bottled-up feelings. I felt attuned to God, keenly aware of his presence and of those around me. I could function this way and have a beautiful life, more beautiful than the life I had known before.

When I went to bed that night before the doctor's appointment, I prayed again. "Lord, I'm beginning to think you have a purpose for this whole thing. I love what is happening in my life and in the lives of those around me, so I have to trust you, Lord. If you want me quiet for a short time or forever, I want to serve you. I can see you working in my life. I can feel you working in my life. I can feel your love. I yield to whatever purpose you have for me and I trust you with my life, even if I have no voice. Amen." I really did feel that I could handle being a mute, but since I didn't have to, I can't say how I would have come through it.

But the willingness was there. The acceptance was there. Maybe that's what God wants. It wasn't just resignation: "Well, if I have to live this way, I guess I can." It was more than just being willing to put up with it. I felt tremendously challenged and excited about the possibilities I was uncovering. I could accept it, as one would accept a gift.

I am confident, as I write this, that my healing began at the moment of my accepting God's will for my life. I felt healthy and whole that night, as though everything in me was in harmony and balance with the entire universe. I believe the releasing of what was bottled up in me (which I am convinced was the source of my throat problems), and the infilling of the Spirit of God into my life to a greater degree than ever before were what healed me.

Morning came, and after the usual routine of breakfast and sending the boys and Dan off, I began to get ready for the visit to my doctor. I was eager for him to see me, not because of what he might say, but because every time he'd ever seen me I was so depressed and down. I was anxious for him to see me happy and radiant.

When he examined my throat, he had some of the same wrinkles on his forehead, but this time they were from disbelief (but I didn't know that yet). He couldn't figure out how he had made such a mistake. When he finished, he said, "Mrs. Zakich, I certainly hope I didn't worry you with what I said." I was afraid even to try to process that statement so I just stared at him blankly and waited for him to speak again. "Mrs. Zakich, your throat has healed perfectly and I think it's all over. You should be able to talk now." I couldn't think of one thing to say. I sat there and continued to stare, almost afraid to believe it. Afraid *not* to believe it. He went on talking and his words sounded as if they were echoing across a big canyon. "You'll probably experience some difficulty since you haven't used your voice box for three months. Your vocal chords have some scar tissue on them so you may sound a little husky for a while . . ." I shook my head to see if I was dreaming. "You may need to have some voice therapy, but everything looks fine. You may not want to talk right now, but just know that whenever you want to, you can begin."

Everything was spinning. I felt lightheaded as I floated out of the office and instinctively found my parked car. "I can talk! I can talk!" I shouted in my mind.

Strange to get into the car and begin my drive home on the freeway, alone, without anyone to tell. It was awhile before I opened my mouth and heard my new voice. So many things were bubbling up into my mind. What did this whole thing mean? Part of me was shouting, "O God, thank you, thank you for healing me and giving me back my voice!" Another part of me was saying, "Don't trust it. Don't get your hopes up. You'll just be more disappointed if it doesn't work." "Lord, why did I have to go through all of this?"

Almost all the way home I had that hassle going on inside me. I was afraid to try to speak, for fear nothing would come out. I stopped at a traffic light, the longest light I ever waited at. The realization that it seemed unusually long brought me back to earth, or at least to an awareness that I was on it. I found myself looking around at the cars on either side and in front of me. Then I looked into the rear view mirror. I stretched my neck until I could see myself in the mirror. I opened my mouth, took a deep breath, and said, "Hello." It came out! I heard it! I can talk! I wanted to shout to the people around me, but the light changed and traffic began to move.

As I drove into our driveway, I paused for a moment to collect myself. "O Father, don't let me forget what I have learned. Lord, I need you again, this time to help me reenter the mainstream of life. Help me to do it wisely. Amen."

And so I began living a more normal lifestyle, but with added knowledge, wisdom, and experience—and of course, being more filled with the Spirit of God than I'd ever been. I started out with kind of a whisper, but each day my voice grew stronger.

It was glorious to be able to talk to my family, but I wasn't so eager to spread the word to those outside my family circle. At first I couldn't figure out why. It seemed strange to realize that I could now talk to all my friends and have to admit that our relationships were better and more fulfilling than they had been before. Did I want to risk blowing it?

I feared that everyone would go back to the old way of relating, with all the superficial chitchat and joking. I didn't want to start spending endless hours on the phone talking about people and family problems. People had finally gotten used to my being silent and, contrary to what I imagined, I didn't feel a great need to tell everything that had gone on in my mind during the three months. During that first month I had tried desperately to remember every thought so I could fill people in on everything when I got my voice back. Now it didn't matter. I prayed over and over for God to show me how I could use this experience in my new life, whatever style it took.

What a wonderful and awesome feeling to realize that I could choose my lifestyle. Always before it had seemed that it chose me. Life happened, and I wasn't aware of having choices. I would wake up each day and there would be certain problems to solve, certain predicaments to deal with. I always felt as if I was reacting and could never get ahead of it.

Here I sat after regaining my voice, realizing I could choose to "happen to life." I could choose whether I wanted to stay at home and read or study, or make little games for friends, or whatever. I could go back to the inner-city ghetto or back to the speaking routine, which I had loved. I could write poetry, become an artist or a musician.

What a heavy responsibility. I wouldn't be able to complain as much, or blame others or circumstances for the things I got myself into. I decided I needed to move slowly, and with much thought and prayer, as I came back out into the world of verbal expression.

I continued to spend a lot of time alone. I made more Tell It Like It Is games and got more and more enthusiastic as I received letters from people requesting them. Some went

to schoolteachers, some to psychologists, some to ministers and youth leaders. Many went to family members who
wanted to improve communication at home. What a joy to
go to the mailbox each day and find letters reporting
positive change in people's lives.

CHAPTER 18

In a matter of weeks, however, I began to feel burdened by the number of game requests coming in. I was forced to work way into the night to complete them. It got so I put off going to the mailbox for fear there would be more orders and then I would be even more behind. "Lord! Why do I always feel tricked? Things start out slowly and I think they're blessings. Then they get bigger and bigger and I never know how to keep them under control. I'm afraid they'll engulf me. Help, Lord!"

It began to take all my time, around the clock. I didn't know how to refuse or how to decide whom to turn down—partly because I was so ecstatic that I had found such a wonderful way to minister to people. I knew the need was so great, and also I liked the glory of getting letters that affirmed me in ways I'd never been affirmed before.

But I was beginning to tire and be impatient with my family if their needs interfered with my painting spools or drawing gameboards. Something would have to give, if my own family was to survive this.

How could I get someone else to make them for me? Maybe I could get a game company to pay me for the idea and just turn it over to them.

I had to learn a whole new vocabulary in order even to

think of things like that. I had never used the words
produce, manufacture, copyright, market, or *vendors* before
(they never appeared in any recipe in Betty Crocker's
cookbook) but here I was having to find out about them.

I started by going to a toy store and copying the names
of companies on the ends of game boxes. I went home and
began to write personal letters to each one, explaining my
whole story and asking if they'd be interested in producing and marketing such a game. Sometimes I would send a
sample game and other times I would draw a detailed
picture of it. It took ten days to write to all the names I'd
copied.

One by one, if the company responded at all, I got
rejections. Each one was like the teacher grading my paper
with a red pencil. I had given birth to a "baby" and people
were saying it was ugly or wouldn't amount to anything. I
got comments like, "No one would be interested in a
noncompetitive game," and, "Whoever heard of a game
where people talk about feelings? People don't want to do
that." "It doesn't sound fun and that's what sells." Some
companies would send a form letter and others would go
into great detail as to why it was no good.

My heart would sink each time I read one, and gradually
I gave up on the game companies. It occurred to me that
maybe only certain kinds of people would enjoy this kind
of game, but who were they? Maybe people interested in
psychology. I'd been reading lately about encounter groups
and places like Esalen, where people go to get in touch
with their feelings.

I bought a copy of *Psychology Today* magazine and
wrote to the editors. I sent them copies of "testimonials"
from those who'd benefited from playing it. They wrote
back and said it was obviously an adult game and there
was no market for serious adult games. Also, to their
knowledge, no one was producing or requesting anything
of the sort. That was my final rejection. I quit writing.

I still had the problem—and now it was bigger—of not
knowing what to do with nearly 100 game orders and only
twenty-four hours in a day. Many of my friends tried to
talk me into starting my own company and producing

them myself. It sounded good, but I didn't know the first thing about how to start. Where do you get gameboards made? Where do you buy little markers? I had exhausted my own and my friends' supply of spools. Where do you get decks of cards printed? And collated? How about boxes? I'd been delivering the homemade games in brown grocery bags. I didn't even know where to buy dice.

The next few months were the most exasperating, humiliating, exhausting, horrible months of my life. I spent days trying to understand language that didn't seem like English. Patent attorneys, printers, box manufacturers, plastic companies, loan companies. Nobody wanted my business because I wanted to make up only about 100 the first time. Dan had been laid off his job and we couldn't afford any more expenses.

I got so I hated to go out with my little gameboard. I hated to make phone calls because I could never seem to explain my problem over the phone. Everyone who saw it shook their head and said, "Why don't you go home and just keep making them for your friends?" At the end of one particularly frustrating day, I put my few sample games under my bed, stuffed the unfilled orders into my kitchen drawer, and decided to forget it.

A year went by. I tried hard to put the whole thing out of my mind. If I received a letter, I thought, "It's nice that the games I used to make are helping people." I began to build a callus around my heart again, because I didn't know how to deal with this. I didn't know where God fit in. I was afraid to ask, for fear he wanted me to learn about the business world. I wanted nothing to do with it.

I began to pretend that I had forgotten about God, probably inwardly feeling that he'd forgotten me. I didn't pray anymore. I couldn't allow myself to feel, because too many things had built up. I was uncomfortable if I saw someone who'd ordered a game four months ago and wondered where it was. I didn't know how to tell them why I quit the game business. Dan was off work for the entire year, so I couldn't have afforded to buy the supplies even if I had wanted to. I felt guilty about the money I had spent so freely to keep everyone supplied with games for so long.

I felt plastic again. One Sunday a friend came up to me at church and invited me to attend a class in her place. It was an eight-week course in Parent/Child Relationships offered by a psychologist, and her tuition had already been paid. Now she found she couldn't attend. I had the time, and I felt the relationships around our house could use some strengthening.

It's amazing to me, as I look back to that time, how I lapsed into the old person I'd been. It had happened gradually as feelings built up in me that I didn't share. I was all bottled-up again. I was unable to feel anything or relate to another person's problems. I didn't feel love coming in or going out. None of my friends or relatives had understood the things I was trying to do to get the game produced, but that hadn't kept them from constantly giving me advice. Everybody was telling me how to run my business, but they were never there with any help or money when I needed them. When I would tell them that something didn't work, they'd give me more advice. I had to turn off.

I never found anyone who would listen to my feelings of frustration, my hurt feelings when I felt rejected, my anger at my ignorance, my fear that God was not in it. I didn't know where I got off the path or how to get back on. There didn't seem to be anybody to share with who could understand the problems I was having.

Anyway, I went to the class and found out on the first day that it was made up of school psychologists, social workers, and counselors. I was embarrassed when they asked me to share my name and occupation. I felt out of place with all those professionals. I sat in the last row each week and never said anything the whole eight weeks.

It was a teacher-training course and it was assumed that each person completing the course would offer it as part of his or her job. I loved what the class was teaching. In fact, it seemed strangely familiar, as if I had heard this stuff before. We learned how to communicate more effectively. We learned listening skills and how to verbalize a message without using code. When the instructor stressed the importance of labeling and expressing feelings, I knew where I had learned it: during my silence. The course verified many of my own discoveries.

Near the end of the eight weeks the instructor asked if we felt ready to start our own classes. There was an interesting discussion about how to get a group together and how to break the ice so that people would share with each other. Someone asked, "How do you get people to warm up to each other so they'll share?" Someone else chimed in with, "Yeah, that's the toughest part, that first time together." Another said, "I feel like I lose a week or two of teaching time while I wait for the group to loosen up and be willing to talk . . . " Then a women suggested, "There ought to be a game or something that could do that." Inside my head I yelled, "There is a game that can do that!" But it never came out of my mouth until after class.

I waited around for everyone to leave so I could talk to the teacher alone. I had never spoken to her and I felt like a little kid wanting to show her a completed assignment but afraid it's not good enough. I was nervous as I introduced myself and beat around the bush for several minutes. Then I said, "You know, I've made a simple little game. It's sort of dumb, but it seems to work for some people. It gets them talking about their feelings. It's nothing special, just some questions and this board with some pictures and stuff on it." I heard myself down-playing it as though I was preparing myself in case she patted me on the head and said, "That's nice."

Instead she said, "Why don't you bring it to class next week and explain it? Maybe the others would like to get one."

I went home with mixed emotions. Sort of excited. Sort of scared. Feeling a need to be cautious so as not to get hurt again.

I dug a game out from under my bed, dusted it off, and took it the following week to the final class of the series. The instructor, Mrs. Rivét, called on me. I was relieved that she hadn't forgotten. Very nervously I placed the gameboard on the floor in front of the class. I didn't look up the entire time of my detailed explanation of the hows

and whys of Tell It Like It Is. My little pictures on the
board looked so childish. The lines making up the road
were so wiggly.

When I finished there wasn't a sound. I eventually
looked up and they were just staring at me. Someone
broke the silence with "Where can we get one of these?"
Someone else said, "Yes, I'd like several." "Me too."
"Send around a clipboard so we can sign up." "When will
they be ready?"

I went home with forty orders, which I added to the
orders in my kitchen drawer. Now I really had problems.

The next day I called the instructor and asked if I could
talk to her. She invited me to her home and I was there
within twenty minutes. I felt foolish as I walked up to her
door. I didn't really know what I wanted to talk to her
about except that I needed help. It helped me to relax
when she told me to call her "Betts" and fixed me a cup
of tea.

I began, "Betts, I just don't know what to do. I've tried
every way I know how to produce these games faster than
the eight hours it takes me to put together each one. I'm
baffled as to how I can fill the orders I have." She listened
as I shared my fears of going to any more printers because
I didn't know the language they seemed to speak. I told of
my embarrassing and sad experiences.

She let me pour out all my frustrations about the business world before she said, "Rhea, I'll go with you! We've
got to get this game produced. There's a need for it. I can
see it, and all the people in the class could see it last
night. Let's just go do it!"

She took my hand, and we proceeded to go all over
town exploring and examining possibilites. She had an
energetic and optimistic spirit that nurtured my tired with-
drawn one. We talked to all kinds of people and were
given leads. We went to places I would never have
thought of.

Eventually we ended up at Goodwill Industries and
visited the print shop where handicapped people learn the
art of typesetting and printing. We talked to the head of
the print shop and asked him if he'd like to print a game.

He said they'd never done anything like a game before, "But letterheads and envelopes *do* seem to get boring for the students. Maybe they could use a challenge like this." He went on to say that he wasn't sure how they would come out. The trainees would have to typeset, print, cut, and collate all the decks of cards, etc., so it might take a couple of weeks. Hooray! I thought. We're in business.

Goodwill printed 100 copies of the game on paper, and Betts and I set out to find where we could get cardboard to mount it on. To assemble the complete game, we needed sheets of cardboard, boxes for the deck of cards and playing pieces made from wooden dowels cut into one-inch pieces, and plastic dice. That presented a problem. Dan had been out of work for nearly a year and we were almost drained of our savings. I couldn't ask him for money to finance this project (which to him seemed like a hobby of mine), so once again I turned to God. Why was I always on this roller coaster with my faith? I now felt encouraged to pray because I was sure that God had led me to Betts Rivét. "OK, Lord, it looks like the game is going to happen now . . . if I can afford the supplies. Help me, Lord, to know where it's going to come from."

CHAPTER 19

I continued to follow the leads and make phone calls,
trying to find the best prices for the parts we needed. Then
a strange thing happened. Someone had given me the
name of a man who worked at a cardboard company, with
the suggestion that he might be able to help us. There was
only one problem: that person didn't know how to reach
him. His name was Jim Hayes, and there were at least
twenty Jim Hayeses in the phone book. It wasn't fun to
call down the list and ask whoever answered if the man of
the house made cardboard boxes. Some people thought I
was doing it as a joke. Others simply said "No" and hung
up.

Then the miracle happened. I had one more name to call
and I was tired and depressed that my time hadn't been
more fruitful. I dialed a number and reached a woman
who told me I had the wrong number when I asked for a
Jim Hayes. Then she said, "Wait a minute. Did you say
Jim Hayes?" I said, "Yes, he works for a cardboard company and I'm trying to locate him. I'm sorry I troubled you."
"This is strange," she said, "but he and his wife are in a
social club with my husband and me."

"Are you sure *that* Jim Hayes works for a cardboard
company?" I asked.

"Yes, I know he does." She seemed so friendly that I

shared my joy and surprise at having a wrong number phone call turn out to be the key to locating this person. I told her why I was wanting to talk to him and our conversation went on for nearly an hour.

I went to bed that night, planning to call him first thing in the morning. I thanked God for the unusual course of events and fell asleep.

I was awakened at seven A.M. by the doorbell. Who on earth could that be? Nobody comes to our house at seven A.M. I grabbed my robe and made my way to the door, rubbing my eyes (I'm always sleepiest right before my alarm goes off). "Special Delivery letter for Rhea Zakich," a young man said. I signed for it and couldn't imagine who it would be from. I opened it and did not recognize the name.

I slowly read, "Dear friend, This is *His* money. I'd like for you to use it for the wonderful game you told me about on the telephone. If you can pay it back someday, fine. If not, that's all right. It belongs to God and He wants me to give it to you." Folded in the letter was a check for $500. I shook my head to see if I was dreaming. It was for real. O God, how could I ever doubt that you would help me if I ask? Why do I stray from you when I know that?

With that money we paid for the printing and the other necessary things for the first batch of 100 games when they came off the press at Goodwill Industries. Those were sold before we finished gluing them to the cardboards. We ordered another 100 and with the help of a flyer announcing the game's availability, those were also sold.

Betts and I were beginning to tire of painting six different colored pegs in each game, 200 games. There we were in our own game business, but it wasn't easy. I still didn't function too well in the business world.

My husband casually asked me one day if it had ever occurred to me that I should be paying sales tax for the games I'd sold. "*Paying* it?" I said. "I'm not *charging* it." He suggested I go to the Board of Equalization and find out how to handle selling and sales tax. How ridiculous not to have thought of something like that, and I never would have known whom to contact to find out about it.

I *had* been charging for the games, at least the last
hundred (the first 100 I had given away). But I hadn't kept
any records and I had changed the price many times
depending on whether I needed to buy paint or more
cardboard. As I recall, I even raised it slightly the time I
wanted to buy something from the Avon Lady. So I made
an appointment to talk to someone about how to handle
my tax obligations.

When I went, I couldn't answer the questions they
asked. I didn't have a business license. I'd have to apply
for a business license and get a resale number. I would
have to file several reports, pay certain fees, etc. It seemed
overwhelming for one who never handled the money in
the household.

I went home to think it over and to try to set up some
sort of bookkeeping system. I spent days trying to remember how many games I'd sold at what price.

One day when I was up to my neck in paperwork, I got
a phone call from Goodwill saying they could no longer
do the game papers for me, because they were having to
take on a new project. I was left with having to find
another place to do the printing.

My confidence had built up quite a bit with the success
of my little kitchen operation. I could now think in bigger
numbers and therefore be more appealing to a printer.

I found a professional printer who would print 300
copies for me, so I placed the order and in three days
picked up a stack of beautiful green and orange shiny
papers to be mounted. The slick paper seemed to look
more classy and I was excited. I couldn't pay the exorbi-
tant price when I saw the bill, so he agreed to bill me,
although it was against their policy. I figured I'd have to
sell these fast and, of course, at a higher price than any of
the previous ones. The orders had been coming in steadily
so I knew that the money was waiting for me as soon as I
could get these games assembled and delivered. I wanted
to do them up nicely, so I decided to invest in better boxes
and have a fancy label that said "Tell It Like It Is" on it.

Someone told me about a new kind of glue that came in
a spray can, which would certainly make the gluing go

faster. I located a firm that sold it by the case only, so I paid $30 for a case. After all, I was going to be in business for a long time. I had gone through $500 and had now soaked in another $500 (the bills to come due next month). I didn't think it would be a problem since I intended to sell the newest ones for five dollars apiece.

Disaster struck. I spent hours one evening trying to figure out the forms for going into business, and trying to bring my records up to date. I hadn't saved receipts or kept track of anything so I became more and more frustrated. About midnight, I tabled the paperwork and decided to glue some gameboards so I could go to bed with some feeling of accomplishment anyway. I laid fifty gameboards all over my kitchen and family room floors. What a neat idea, I thought; I'll mass produce these by spraying all these boards and then I'll smooth the beautiful game papers in place and tomorrow I'll have a whole stack of games ready to go. I did that and felt productive enough to call it a night, so I went to bed. I tossed and turned, worrying how to handle the accounting part of my business, but finally fell asleep with the comforting thought that in the morning I could package fifty games.

In the morning I walked into the kitchen to receive the biggest shock ever! The gameboards had curled up like giant potato chips. They were ruined. I tried to flatten them but they cracked. The glue had been too wet or something, $250 lost! I was sick.

I looked at the sight and didn't know how to express what I was feeling. That batch of games represented the money that was to pay the debts I'd run up. Dan still wasn't working. I couldn't imagine how we would pay the bills when they came. That does it! That's the last straw. I give up. God! I don't understand you! Where do you go when I need you?

I cried as I stacked the curled boards up and stomped them in my trash barrel. A part of me died that day as I decided to go out of business.

CHAPTER 20

Because I couldn't express my sadness to anyone, it came out of me as anger. I cleaned my kitchen and living room, removing all traces of the game business. I sprayed floral scented perfume around to cancel out the glue and paint smell my family had gotten used to. I was abrupt with everyone and everything as I tried to pretend that it didn't matter. Under my breath I was muttering, "All right God, I quit! If you want this game out in your world, you do it! I was willing to help you, but there must be something I'm doing wrong or something I don't understand, so count me out!"

My family was shocked when I announced that I had gone out of the game business, but they didn't complain. For the first time in months, they could walk through a room without having to step over stacks of uncollated cards, gameboards with glue drying, freshly painted pegs, and stacks of empty boxes. And they could breathe more freely, too.

After a few days, there wasn't a mention of the game. I was so sure that God was going to be sorry he didn't help me that I could act as if I didn't care until he got in touch with me again.

A young boy from our neighborhood noticed the crinkled gameboards awaiting trash pickup and decided to help himself to one. Since I had also thrown out all the other ingredients, he was able to get a complete set of everything necessary to play Tell It Like It Is. His mother, a nursing instructor, looked it over and decided that it would fit nicely in her nursing program. She saw it as a way to take students beyond medical terminology and sterile procedures and help them learn to relate to patients' feelings and perhaps to their coded messages.

She used the game with her nursing students with amazing results. The students seemed to become more sensitive to each other *and* to their patients after they engaged in it for awhile. The instructor was excited about this crude, handmade game, so she asked her son where he had gotten it. He reported that it had been destined for the trash pickup down the street at the Zakiches.

I didn't know his mother, although I had seen her a few times in her front yard and usually gave a neighborly wave as I drove by. I had no way of knowing that she had recently joined with a young man in a partnership to produce medical teaching aids. Their company was one mile from my house. She showed it to her partner, and the two of them saw great potential in it.

Needless to say, I was startled to receive a phone call from a stranger asking if I'd ever considered putting my game on the market. I thought it was a joke. One of my friends pulling my leg, perhaps. I tried to control myself and act cool. "Oh, I *thought* about it, but I don't really think I'll do any more with it." I was afraid to get excited because I didn't want to be hurt anymore.

He went on to say, "Seriously, I think this game has tremendous possibilities and I'd like to talk to you about marketing it." It began to penetrate that this man was serious.

"Where are you located?" I asked in response to his suggesting that we get together to discuss it. I couldn't get over the fact that I'd written so many letters to companies all over the country, and here were these people almost in my backyard asking *me* if they could produce and market my game. I had *begged* the other places. It all seemed strange, but I consented to meet Mr. Herndon.

Between the phone call and our getting together, I had time to call several of my friends and share my excitement. Instead of rejoicing with me, however, they all became suspicious. They warned me about people who steal ideas and capitalize on them. "Look out for him," they cautioned. "He's going to rip you off." "Don't let him take advantage!" "You'd be smart if you made him pay a real high price for that game!" "Don't let him copyright it in his name." I hadn't thought of *any* of those things. And I didn't tell my friends that I had thrown the entire idea out in the trash a few days before.

As I drove to the office where Au-Vid Inc. was located, I felt their suspicion seep into me. What if he is trying to take advantage? Should I tell him I want to get paid for the idea? Is the idea really *mine* after I threw it in the trash? I remembered my words with God when I was angry about the curled gameboards. Is this God's way of responding? I arrived at the address, took a deep breath, and said a short prayer asking God to give me wisdom and to remove the suspicion from me.

The moment I stepped inside that office, I knew I was in the right place. It felt like home to my spirit. There was instant rapport between Mr. Herndon and me. I knew I could trust him. He told me again how excited he was about the possibilities he saw in Tell It Like It Is, and I in turn shared my briefcase full of letters from persons who'd had a life-changing experience and had taken time to write.

Excitement rose as we went through the letters one by one and marveled at all that had happened. One in particular spoke to him. A professional businessman wrote, "My teen-age daughter and I hadn't talked for about a year, but last night with your game we were able to really communicate. I love my daughter and was able to tell her so for the first time in years. Thank you for creating such a wonderful tool. P.S. Tell It Like It Is should *never* be called a game because it's NOT a game! It's more of a non-game!" We continued to read, and time and time again someone said "Don't call this beautiful experience a 'game.'"

Mr. Herndon gathered several of his staff together, and all of us played for about an hour. By the end of the time, it hit us: It's not a game, it's an UNGAME®! It looks like a game, but what it seems to do is enable persons to relate to each other *without* playing the games so common in communication. The UNGAME®. We all liked the sound of it, so my "baby" was christened with a new name. I felt as if I had put it in a foster home where it would be better cared for. We drew up a contract.

That night as I went to bed, I again marveled at how God seems to come through in my life. I shared my joy with him. "Father, Father. Why do I ever doubt you? Why do I doubt myself? Help me to trust you more. Thank you for teaching me that once I *let go*, you would show me where the game belonged. O God, help me to learn *how* to release and *when* to release."

I spent a lot of time in the coming weeks thinking about releasing. Letting go and letting God. I had heard that phrase many times. Why was it so hard for me? It was revealed to me in a prayer time that my role in many things was to be that of starter, initiator, "creator." Many times it would be someone else's responsibility to take the project to the next step. I could see how I had made life hard for myself by thinking that just because God gave me an idea, he expected *me* to take it all the way to fruition, to completion.

One of the lessons God wanted me to learn is that I need to ask daily what I am to do. I must never run ahead of his directions. If God wants something done, he will see to it that it gets done (and he'll do it more quickly if we don't stand in his way). When I am finished with my part of something I must set it free, so that the next person can fulfill his or her purpose in it.

From that day on, my life has been a series of new adventures. A few months after our meeting, Au-Vid Inc. came out with the UNGAME®. In a matter of months it began to spread across the United States and even into foreign countries. As I write this, seven years after the first UNGAME® came off the press, nearly half a million have sold throughout the world. It is translated into different languages.

"Thank you, Lord! Thank you for creating something through me. For helping (allowing?) me to get into a position of being open and receptive to your creating through me. I know, Lord, I cannot take the credit for this. Forgive me if I brag and say, 'Look what I did!' when I know in my heart that I couldn't have done it without you. Remind me, Lord, when I forget, that *all* praise and glory are yours."

My life has been full of correspondence in the past few years. I never tire of reading the stories of miracles in relationships, new awareness, deepened understanding. Many may not even realize why they get up from the table and say, "Wow, that's great! I feel so good." But I have an idea they've experienced pouring out some of their muddy water, making room for the pure, refreshing water of the Spirit. They've experienced healing.